EXCERPTS FROM COMMON SENSE 2.0

Seriously addressing the wealth concentration problem Thomas Piketty uncovers requires political reform centered in political equality, and that is what this book is all about. (page 29)

The Washington DC metro area has the highest median income and the 3 wealthiest counties in the US, but also has the highest rate in the US (>30%) for childhood food insecurity (i.e., poverty). This sounds more "third world" gated community than world super power. (page 30)

All this money is a windfall to our "watchdog" media, to the extent they become coopted to big money in politics under the guise of "free speech" (i.e., our watchdog media has become a lapdog to big money). (page 32)

Jack Abramoff is a former Washington DC lobbyist . . . casually suggest they join their lobbying firm after "public service" . . . "the moment I said that to them or any of our staff said that to them, that was it, we owned them."   One could call this preemptive bribery, and it's the air DC breathes.   (page 44)

The S&L crisis did result in over 800 criminal convictions. Contrast this with the more current 2008 / 2009 near apocalyptic financial meltdown where there have been a miniscule number of criminal convictions. Do we not have politically connected elites who are not subject to the law? Do we not have a government that does not enforce laws and regulations, because it does not want to appear anti- business since this would dry up political funding? Has too big to fail been expanded to include too big to jail? (page 63)

So what brings us here as humans some 14 billion years after the biggest balloon pop (big bang) of all time? Complex adaptive systems science provides the answer. (page 69)

Over the past 30 years China's annual economic growth rate has been about 3 times that of the US, translating into a corresponding improvement in the living standards of its people. . . . The Chinese governing process is not unlike the extensive use of advisory referendums, and internet feedback, acted upon by a Board of Directors from a long term goal driven, strategic point of view. (page 85)

Religion can be viewed as a check and balance to counter laws that are less than moral. (page 102)

"Directed eDemocracy" comes from an eclectic selection of best democratic processes from around the world. "Directed eDemocracy" also has a solid scientific grounding coming from "Complex Adaptive Systems" science. (page 107)

In this Internet Age, we also have the opportunity of using new tools to create a Directed eDemocracy where citizens are not just consumers, but co-creators of government content. (page 129)

To solve problems, compete, excel, and lead in this globalized internet age we want a government that is set up to provide the best cognition and adaptability possible for all stakeholders. Beyond that we do not want to let the personality of our government default to something we really don't want as a society. In effect Directed eDemocracy changes the personality of our government. We have "opened it up", and moved it out of the money'd special interest closed confines of Washington, and improved networked connections to all voters.   (page 130)

PREFACE – COMMON SENSE 2.0

THOMAS PAINE & THOMAS PREUSSER

Thomas Paine wrote Common Sense to bolster the American Revolution. Beyond having the same first name and last initial, I see many parallels between Thomas Paine and myself. Paine was a knowledge and idea explorer, with a wide range of interests and pursuits, including corset maker, tax collector, school teacher, businessman, magazine editor, bridge designer, inventor, and philosopher. My own interests and pursuits have included science, mathematics, business, finance, computer systems, and philosophy. My knowledge and idea exploration into government started with the observation that the US has a lot of governing problems, yet virtually no one is "looking under the hood" to see what is fundamentally and structurally wrong with the mechanics of our governing engine / system. My exploration took me not only to looking at best governing practices around the world, but also those practices that had grounding in the modern science of "Complex Adaptive Systems".

In the first six chapters of this book I discuss various problems that our current governmental system seems incapable of addressing. **In those first six chapters I also get somewhat into solutions to those problems, but that is not my intent in writing this book. My intent is to present, in the final five chapters of this book, a simple implementable change, Directed eDemocracy, to our US governmental system that will improve both the quality of governmental "cognition", and the process of governmental problem solving.** Although written with the US in mind, much of what is in this book is applicable to the rest of the world.

When writing Common Sense in 1775, Paine chose to write clearly and concisely, as opposed to the formal learned style of the day. I have also chosen to write clearly and concisely, as opposed to the "academic" style of many of the works that I read prior to my writing Common Sense 2.0. I have also chosen to write this book in a "wide ranging", "networked", "synthesized", and "holistic" style which is most evident by my use of highlighted blocks of text. This style is most analogous to the style of "new" media web pages, such as those used by the Huffington post. A particular challenge was presenting a "thumbnail sketch" of the new science of "Complex Adaptive Systems" as it relates to government. **"Complex Adaptive System Science" is the multidisciplinary study of networks of interactions which reflects both the importance of self (individualism), and the importance of the networked ecosystem of "selfs" (common good). Paine envisioned a society based on individualism and the common good, where ordinary people can make sound judgements on their governance. I totally agree with that, and in Common Sense 2.0 I present Directed eDemocracy to carry that thinking into the Internet Age. Directed eDemocracy relates to using the Internet as a tool of governance to give all voters direct interaction with government, thereby curbing the disproportionate influence of money'd special interests over entrenched political elites.**

My special thanks to my wife Cathy and all friends and acquaintances who helped with this book.

"If voting made any difference they wouldn't let us do it." - Mark Twain

CHAPTER 1

POLITICAL INEQUALITY &

POLITICAL ELITES

American democracy struggles at the start of a global cultural revolution called the Internet Age. The early days of the internet were called the Web 1.0 days where most users, like drivers on a one way street, were consumers of web content and not content creators. We have now advanced to what is called Web 2.0, where with facilities such as Facebook, Twitter, YouTube, and Huffington Post, **we users are not only content consumers, but also content creators**. We are drivers on a two way street which is a more engaged, dynamic, and collaborative global community, and ecosystem. Web 2.0 concepts have, and will continue, to change the world and democratic systems in evolutionary ways.

> The Huffington Post was incubated in 2005 by a small group of innovative and entrepreneurial journalists wanting to create a "New Media" at the intersection of content and technology. Starting with a rolodex of personal contacts,

At the beginning of the American Revolution Thomas Paine wrote a pamphlet called Common Sense which called for a distinctly American political identity rooted in constitutional representative democracy. According to Paine colonial rule was lopsided in favor of remotely cloistered political elites whose interests, mainly monetary, were different and contrary to that of the general American populace. Paine also saw a big problem of responsiveness when the interactivity of government is controlled by the speed of a ship, which typically meant it took one year to receive a response to any petition.

Paine's pamphlet made Common Sense to the American populace and bolstered the revolution and American constitutional representative democracy. That democracy however, is Common Sense 1.0, which like Web 1.0 sets up American citizens on essentially a non-interactive one way street. **We are consumers of "two sizes fit some" political party platforms proffered every two year election cycle.**

We still have cloistered political elites whose interests are often different and contrary to that of the general American populace and aligned with money'd special interests. **Responsiveness, if any, is no longer dictated annually by the speed of a ship but perhaps perversely, by an even longer two year or four year election cycle where we as voters "consume" one of two gridlocked political party platforms, and then basically go away until the next election cycle.**

➢ Founding Father John Adams foresaw the current environment when he wrote: "We may please ourselves with the prospect of free and popular governments. But there is great danger that those governments will not make us happy. God grant that they may. But I fear that in every assembly, members will obtain an influence by noise not sense. By meanness, not greatness. By ignorance, not learning. By contracted hearts, not large souls." **In recent times the public's approval rating of Congress sank to an all-time low of less than 10%. I would dare say that during American Revolutionary times King George III's approval rating was similar.**

➢ In 1776 America literacy rates were 95% for men and 60% for women. Despite these high literacy rates the founding fathers distrusted the "workability" of direct popular vote. At the onset of American representative democracy, House Representatives were elected by direct popular vote, but only propertied white men could vote. Senators were elected by state legislatures and the President was elected by electors selected by state legislatures. The President to this day is elected by the Electoral College and not direct popular vote. Since the Electoral College is an amalgamation of 50 states, the winner by nationwide popular vote can still lose the election. This happened most recently in the 2016 Trump versus Clinton presidential election. In this environment, "gaming" the Electoral College system means big money focusing on a few swing states to influence the election. Political games also pervade current presidential primaries where large numbers of political party elites, including Republican Party elites but more blatantly numerous Democratic party elites, can vote at presidential nominating conventions irrespective of voter preferences in prior presidential primaries. **Indeed in retrospect, the founding fathers and current career politicians biggest failure was and is to institutionalize political inequality addressed first via civil war and extension of the vote to male blacks, and subsequently to women. The current battle is to make popular vote actually count, and in a bigger context, to make congress responsive to other than political elites and big money.**

American democracy is essentially working as intended when set up more than 200 years ago - and that is the problem. Over those years a lot has changed in the world, yet only 17 constitutional amendments beyond the initial 10 bill of rights amendments have been passed. Most notable have been amendments dealing with political inequality. At the onset, when no taxation without representation was the rallying cry, only propertied white men who paid taxes were allowed to vote. Subsequently voting was expanded in fits and starts to blacks and women. But voting in an election every couple of years does not constitute political equality. In fact between elections an army of money'd lobbyists representing special interests are exerting political power while the average citizen becomes an afterthought with nil political power until the next election cycle.

> Isn't it finally time for political equality to be added to the Bill of Rights? How many disruptive internal conflicts (civil war, suffragette, civil rights, corporatist) do we have to fight to put this to rest? Should not our once proud, now delusional democracy stop it's decline into money'd oligarchy by sharing the expectation of political equality? **The right to political equality means the right of all citizens to "a level playing field" for ongoing, interactive, and real time dialogue with a government which is open and transparent.**

> In 2014 political scientist's Martin Gilens and Benjamin Page released a data driven analysis showing the US is in effect not a democracy, but an oligarchy where money'd elites hold sway. In this regard the US is not unlike other oligarch controlled "dubious democracies" such as Russia. In such oligarch controlled "dubious democracies" the average citizen has little effect on government policy, while money'd elites have great effect and hold effective veto power.

In some 200 years of effort towards political equality we still have "propertied white men" calling the shots in the form of money'd lobbyists. Those of us who vote generally feel good about it unless the political party product we "consumed" lost. We go away for two or four years and hope for more agreeable results in the future. A large portion of us do not vote because we don't see it making much of a difference. In the time between elections most governing is done by the "political elite / experts" in a less than transparent manner. **How have these "political elite / experts" been doing? - for the average American terrible** (as I will discuss later). In a governmental sense, things have not changed since Thomas Paine wrote Common Sense - we still have "remotely cloistered political elites" controlled by money'd interests with perhaps a "bone" of responsiveness every election cycle.

We can and should do better. Political inequality leads to two sets of rules, winners and losers, and less freedom for the losers. The Supreme Court got it all wrong. Freedom of speech is only part of freedom. The other part of freedom is political equality in the process of making laws that are made with all in mind, or else you have whole classes of people - blacks, women, the poor ..., who are less free and likely to remain marginalized second class citizens.

> ➤ The Progressive Era occurred in the US from about 1890 to 1940 in response to the control of government by political machines and bosses resulting in corruption. Modernization along with effective and efficient government, were major themes of progressives. Progressives sought to put the citizenry more in direct charge of government, with numerous states setting up referendum and initiative processes. The progressive era was also a reaction by small business, farm, and labor interests to the power of monopolistic businesses to dominate with anticompetitive business practices. This led to the Sherman Antitrust Act and more government regulation. Political inequality was also a theme of the Progressive Era resulting in the nineteenth amendment to the Constitution which gave women the right to vote. In many respects the Progressive Era has parallels to the present era including political inequality, "too big" businesses running amok, and government made ineffective and inefficient in an atmosphere of corruption and two party political machines.

> ➤ A revolution in communications has occurred over the past 200 plus years. We have gone from infrequent

communications to a few people at the speed of a horse or ship, to frequent communications to many people at instantaneous internet speeds.   American government however is stuck 200 years back at slow and infrequent (two year election cycles) and few people too few people (congressman to money'd lobbyists between elections). This fuels rising expectations that our slow to react and adapt representative democracy cannot meet in its current form. This of course leads to "big crises of expectations". Political pundits say crisis is the way democracy is supposed to work - i.e., messy and not pretty. **But wouldn't we as citizens prefer dealing with smaller crises rather than big ones? Wouldn't we as citizens prefer governments that can get the job done without giving rise to whole groups of disaffected Occupy Wall Street or Tea Party citizens?**

"There is nothing which I dread so much as a division of the republic into two great parties, each arranged under its leader, and concerting measures in opposition to each other. This, in my humble apprehension, is to be dreaded as the greatest political evil under our Constitution." - John Adams

"The man who moves a mountain begins by carrying away small stones." - Confucius

"Be less curious about people and more curious about ideas." - Marie Curie

CHAPTER 2

JOBS, HEALTH CARE,

& CRONY CAPITALISM

Americans are used to thinking "we are number one". Certainly in the post-apocalyptic WWII era America was number one in a lot of areas, most notably the world of pop culture spread via Hollywood. **Pop culture notwithstanding the facts now often show we are not number one except that we do have perhaps "the best government money can buy".** An analysis by Transparency International ranked the US 19th out of 176 countries for least corruption - not bad but far from number one. **Government corruption driven insidiously by money'd special interests creates two sets of rules, less than free markets, and**

crony capitalism which translates into poor performance in the economy, and in particular poor job creation and health care system performance. Americans tend to think we have the best economic system in all respects, yet in terms of GDP per capita we are sinking out of the top ten and have a shrinking middle class. The rapidly growing Chinese economy is on track to eclipse our own economy as the world's largest. In 2008 the World Economic Forum ranked the US first for global economic competitiveness. We have since slipped out of the top 5 with our grid locked system of government being a major factor.

❯ Social Progress Imperative is an organization whose goal is to improve the lives of people around the world by promoting social progress. Of course to do this you have to develop a measure or index for quality of life that reflects how nations are progressing in relation to each other. The 2014 index was developed by a team headed by Harvard Business Professor Michael Porter and MIT Professor Scott Stern. In the 2014 index the US ranked 70th for Health & Wellness, 41st for Personal Safety, 34th for Water & Sanitation, and 15th for Freedom &Choice.

❯ Following the "Great Recession" the US found itself with persistently high structural unemployment, especially among youth and minorities. This is being mitigated somewhat by vast numbers of baby boomers entering retirement. Some of the structural job loss is due to globalization and loss of manufacturing jobs to emergent countries that have more competitive, lower cost labor. But most overlooked is the current nature of job creation / destruction that is going on. Historically, for example, horse related jobs were replaced with skilled auto related jobs. Increasing skill requirements and "man/machine" productivity gains, fed the growth of the middle class. Fast forward to the computer and internet age and "no man/computer" productivity gains lead to job creation

/ destruction which is skewed towards job destruction. Globalized Darwinian competition puts a premium on entrepreneurial workers that can come up with ideas and innovate. This is a "sports star" environment where few reach the major leagues to be richly rewarded, and the rest are relegated to persistent under or unemployment. An unemployment rate of 5.0% replaces 4.0% as the new norm for "full employment". If one also counts part-time workers who would like full time work and frustrated job seekers who have left the work force in the past year the real unemployment rate is twice the headline number. Following the "Great Recession" the labor participation rate sank to a low not seen since 1978. Stagnant or declining incomes create downward mobility out of the middle class and consumer focus on low cost goods and services which business responds to primarily by "driving labor costs out of the system". So the new ideas and innovations include Walmart with global supply chains sourced mainly from China, Amazon with no need to use a retail sales clerk, Travelocity with no need to use a local travel agent …. Jobs, income, and the middle class disappear never to come back because as economists would say, there are unprecedented structural changes going on in the job market.

Because our government's attention is focused by "drive labor cost out of the system" business lobbying, there must be structural changes in government to get other than same old, same old job initiatives. Just decreasing tax rates when problems in the jobs market are structural will not work - more creative, less ideologue driven policies are required. For example, most businesses would not blink twice about borrowing 30 year money at historically low, less than 4 percent interest rates, to fund needed long term capital expenditures. The idea here is to use cheap money to create assets that will have big paybacks long into the future. In fact this is precisely what China has been doing over the past 30 years to get economic growth rates triple that of the US. Yet our dysfunctional government, despite crumbling infrastructure such as roads and bridges, did not do this, even though this would have boosted the economy and jobs. Rather we got tax cuts and less than effective deficit stimulus spending skewed to the short term, with businesses sitting on cash hoards and not undertaking capital expenditures because they want to see demand turn around first, or they see greater opportunities off shore.

> Free Trade Agreement policies need to be rethought. In 1974 the US President was given authority to "fast track" fair trade agreements. Prior to the mid 1970's the US would typically run both nominal trade deficits and surpluses from one year to the next. Since the mid 1970's it has all been ever larger trade deficits, especially since 2000 when "free trade" was made a cornerstone of the Bush administration. Trade deficits are of course symptomatic of shipping jobs overseas. Presidential "fast track" authority basically cedes control over what is in fair trade agreements to industry and corporate interests. The resulting agreement is dumped to Congressional vote with instructions not to debate, amend, or filibuster. In fact members of Congress don't really know what is in the free trade agreement, but most probably don't care because money'd industry and corporate lobbyists have already secured their votes ahead of time. The economic theory behind free trade is that every country produces the goods and services that it has a natural advantage producing. Greenland should probably not try to produce its own coffee. Through subsequent free trade the consumers in every country benefit from cheaper and better goods and services. While I agree with this theory over the long run, there are global societal problems of adjustment and trade balance over the short run. What jobs do Greenland's now defunct coffee producers find to be able to buy relatively inexpensive trade goods? Should they go into the ice business? This is precisely what we are seeing in the US following prior free trade agreements. We have cheaper

goods and services available, but a displacement of workers who are now pushed into a higher risk, often entrepreneurial environment that will have some winners but many losers. This is not an optimum stable environment in which to raise a family. Government is ill advised to further pursue Free Trade Agreements when unemployment is historically high, and/or personal income is stagnated or even declining. This is especially true when prior Free Trade Agreements have failed to deliver on promises of an abundance of new high paying export related jobs. Actually "Free" is a misnomer, since much of the negotiating in these agreements is done behind closed doors and actually involves sweet deal anticompetitive terms. The forces of corporate big money lobbying should be resisted since it has a very narrow profit focus. The focus should be expanded to include global environment, quality and safety of goods, and the need as a sovereign nation to still be in control of our own security and destiny.

> A major governmental problem is accounting and budgetary gimmickry which feeds a general dysfunction of distrust. Private business, which must use Generally Accepted Accounting Principles, or GAAP, has no such problem. Basically governmental accounting, as practiced, covers up fiscal irresponsibility by recognizing revenue up front while back-loading expense recognition to future periods. The most obvious example of this is the unfunded 100 trillion dollar liability that Social Security and Medicare represent - that's $300,000 per person. In this distrustful environment deficit hawks force us to pass on rational opportunities, such as borrowing 30 year money at less than 4 percent interest to boost jobs and the economy with long term infrastructure projects. This money would of course have to be held in an infrastructure trust so it would not be syphoned off by government as usual (i.e., recent federal increases in the federal gas tax have not gone to the Highway Trust Fund but

towards "deficit reduction"). As part of our checks and balances we need an independent part of government that can think long term and be above accounting and budgetary gimmickry.

➤ Fostering exploration is an important part of government. Columbus of course sailed and discovered America with Spanish government sponsorship. Government sponsorship of exploration also means ideas and innovations which in turn bolster the economy and jobs, witness the internet and GPS (global positioning system). Some would say that the private sector free market based economy provides all the incentive and all the ideas and innovations we need. When the economy is good and jobs plentiful I would have to agree. But that is not always the case, witness the Depression and "Great Recession". The fact is there are different kinds of innovation.   Business innovation, while bolstered by incentives of monetary gain, tends to come with patents and business secrets that detract from follow on networked sharing in the idea / innovation ecosystem.   In contrast government sponsored exploration leads to innovations that are more "open platforms" on which to build a myriad of subsequent economic ventures, witness the internet and GPS. So government certainly has a role in this type of innovation, and it usually relates to supporting basic research performed independently by scientists and engineers at universities and research centers. No one set out to create the internet or GPS - they were sideline byproducts of the networked scientist and engineer ecosystem supported by the government.

➤ A 2014 Brookings report shows US new business formation rates trending steadily downward across all states and metro areas, being about half what it was 30 some years ago. That being said, "small businesses are the job creators" is a much misused statement, perhaps because it is used in the context of justifying cutting taxes to all small business owners. But not all small businesses are equal in creating jobs. A given city supports only so many of the usual real estate, cleaning, retail …, jobs and businesses. Real job growth comes from new innovative products and services and entrepreneurs that will energetically pursue them. Taxes are an afterthought to these driven entrepreneurs unless they make them less competitive, and if they are so vulnerable their products or services are perhaps not that new and innovative in the first place. Exemplary of this are what today are large companies worth billions, which were started in dorm rooms with no capital other than an algorithmic imagination in the minds of geeks. To foster job growth thus means to foster ideas and innovations. Political equality is the place to start since money'd corporate lobbying creates two sets of rules and a less than level playing field that stifles competition and upstarts. Higher education and research should be another area of focus, particularly as concerns our best and brightest. Science in the US is to a large degree not homegrown, since some 50 percent of PHD candidates are foreign born. As globalization progresses more and more of these PHD candidates are going back to their home countries leading to a brain drain. So a final area of continued focus should be freedom, which relates somewhat to stifling over regulation but mainly to freedom of ideas and freedoms that attract the best and brightest immigrants.

In his book Measure of a Nation, Howard Friedman finds that among large developed countries, the US ranks last in life expectancy, yet spends about twice as much per capita on health care costs – and we are only beginning to look at universal health care coverage which other developed countries already have. It costs some $1,500 less to build a car in Canada than it does in the US because of our health care system. Our health care system adversely affects job retention and creation. Our aging population's Medicare requirements will sink our economy in trillions of debt on the current trajectory. The best our government could do concerning this problem was come up with a still bloated non performing health care system with legislation written essentially by special interest lobbyists.

> Expensive health care tied to US employers puts those employers at a global competitive disadvantage. The US as a society becomes second rate when all of our peers provide universal health care and we don't. "Obamacare" is an attempt to address these issues, but it was basically cobbled together and written by money'd health care lobbyists and therefore does little if anything to address the cost problem which is a ticking time bomb. Republicans have proposed vouchering to attack this problem, but this is lobbyist induced delusion since free health care markets do not exist, particularly in less urban areas. Evidence of this is the fact that depending on geographical location, the price of a standard "Obamacare" plan can vary by as much as 300%. As long as money'd lobbyists reign in government we have crony capitalism and less than free markets. Vouchering only serves to shift unwavering high costs to private individuals who lack normal consumer market knowledge and information to make sense of bills which tend to be arcane. Therefore a costly underperforming health care system will likely continue to be a drag on non-health care parts of the US economy and decrease our standard of living.

> Items on lab bill:
> 80051 ELECTROLYTE panel
> 86618 LYME IGG / IGM screen
> 84450 SGOT (AST)
> 87798 EHRLICHA / ANAPLASMA, PCR

> (Could I have fries with that)

The preceding is just a sample of the world of medical billing made arcane perhaps on purpose by an industry trying to protect profits that are outsized by world standards. A hip replacement in the US is seven times more costly than a hip replacement in Belgium. A one month supply of brand name Lipitor in the US costs seventeen times as much as a one month supply of brand name Lipitor in New Zealand. There are a litany of excuses for these higher costs, none of which are supported by the data. Defensive medicine, high pay for doctors and medical practitioners, high administrative costs, and high cost of drugs cumulatively explain less than 20% of the high costs the US has in relation to the rest of the world. The biggest single factor in the high US costs is the amount billed for patient services. In the rest of the developed world these costs are negotiated and billed to a single payer that has real negotiating power. In the US, patients faced with ill health or even death, do not have much negotiating power or inclination, and will pay exorbitant prices. The result is that providers bill as much as they can in a farcical collusive system designed to rake in money for system insiders. In fact the typical medical provider bills more than twice the amount they expect to collect.   A recent California study found hospitals billing almost four times what was collected. Collusive overbilling gives insurance companies pretense to claim over blown negotiating power, and/or over blown payment percentages on behalf of less knowledgeable policy holders.   Patients viewing their insurance company statements may think the insurance company is paying 80% of the amount billed, when in effect the insurance company might be paying less than 20% and the balance is farcical collusive overbilling.   None of the overbilling California hospitals lost money and in fact they all made healthy "profits" yet paid no taxes since they are nonprofits.

> To solve the major problem that health care is, we need only to look at those countries around the world that are near

matches to the US in most respects, but are somewhat further along in solving their own health care issues.

The Swiss, whose life expectancy is second only to that of Japan, have a system very much like "Obamacare". All Swiss citizens are required by law to purchase their own health insurance from private health insurance companies. These insurance companies are to all offer the same basic package of services at no profit. Beyond the basic package insurance companies are free to compete with supplemental plans that expand the basic package. The Swiss government subsidizes health care for the poor, and monthly costs can be tailored somewhat with higher/lower deductibles. Monthly costs can also be reduced by joining an HMO sole provider - otherwise any provider can be used. The government negotiates fixed prices every year for services and medications and thereby the Swiss pay somewhat less than we in the US do for health care, though they are still among the highest cost per capita in the world. The hope is that over time the cost curve will continue to bend downwards via government negotiations and consumer driven elements. Countering this however is the fact that insurance companies and health care providers still operate somewhat like a de facto cartel, so cost continues to be an issue especially since government subsidizes health care for the less well-off and much of the cost has been privatized out of government to consumers. But overall disproportionate costs have not affected Swiss competitiveness in the global economy as they consistently rank at or near the top and ahead of the US which has seen a steady decline in global economic competitiveness. The lesson for the US is that the current "Obamacare" track might be viable, but only if a phase II of major cost containment is undertaken including government negotiated prices on services and medications and abandoning fee for service and going to fee per patient.

➢ Canada is the other country around the world that is a near match to the US in most respects, yet is somewhat further along in solving their own health care issues. **Canada is near Japan at the top of the list for life expectancy among large developed countries while the US is at the bottom. It costs Canada 1/3 less per capita than the US to achieve these results with a system which is set up much like Medicare in the US.** Government run insurance at the provincial level sets prices with private providers. Funding is generally 70% from income taxes and 30% private expenditure via a monthly premium adjusted for the poor. Private insurance companies offer supplemental plans beyond the basic plan. Patients are free to choose their own general practitioner. Physicians are paid fee per visit, and public hospitals have set budgets. Wait times have at times been an issue, but mostly true urgent care has not been a problem. Surveys find the overwhelming majority of Canadians like their system, especially when compared to the US system. The lesson for the US is that this is an excellent alternative available by simple adjustments and improvements to Medicare and expanding it to all over time. Powerful lobbying forces will have to be overcome and from a cost containment perspective we would have to move away from fee for service.

➢ Neither Obamacare nor Medicare has undertaken action on the structural reforms needed in health care delivery to drive cost containment. To be globally competitive we have to cut costs by 1/3 while maintaining the same quality of care. Structural reforms will help somewhat, but it is likely parts of the health care industry will "take a haircut", so the lobby machine is in high gear to resist needed structural reforms. Many Republicans can be expected to flip flop their opposition to Obamacare as they try to "voucherise" a revised Obamacare and propose complete elimination of Medicare by "voucherising" it as well. In a sense this has already started in the form of the Medicare Advantage program which lets Medicare recipients get all their Medicare coverage through private insurance. The Medicare Advantage trade-off for Medicare recipients is a somewhat broader benefits package negotiated by insurance companies with medical service providers who give price breaks to be a sole provider - i.e. limited choice. It is likely that lacking true structural reform in the way medical services are provided, these plans will be cost constrained and become less attractive over time. Thus vouchering only privatizes health care costs that will continue to be high by global standards.

> Mayo Clinic is the largest nonprofit medical group practice in the world. Mayo's quality of care consistently ranks in the top 10 in the US across a broad list of specialties. Mayo does not tie doctor income to fee for service, and all doctors are on a salary that is market based. Consequently costs such as its end of life care costs are half that experienced by its peers. Since some 25% of all medical costs are end of life care costs, this is a very important cost containment category. Market based salaries also allows Mayo to address physician shortages and wait times.

> "Reference pricing" is an attempt by health plans to control costs by focusing price negotiations on numerous and expensive procedures such as knee and hip replacements. CALPERS, which manages benefits for state of California retirees and public employees, has used this with success for years. Under "reference pricing" a health plan sets a price ceiling on what it will pay for a procedure. If a patient selects a provider that charges more than the negotiated price the difference is paid by the patient out of pocket. Experience has shown that this approach, if implemented correctly and reasonably, can control costs while maintaining choice and quality of care.

In summation, our jobs and health care problems show an inability to adapt. In the next four chapters I expand this "Common Sense 2.0" discussion of problems to current US governmental structures. This is in keeping with my intent to concentrate on our governmental adaptive processes, rather than solutions to the actual problems themselves. Following those four chapters are the final five chapters where I present the science of "Complex Adaptive Systems" before moving onto "Directed eDemocracy as an easily implemented solution and paradigm for successful governance in the Internet Age.

"Healthy citizens are the greatest asset any country can have."
- Winston S. Churchill

"The interest of [businessmen] is always in some respects different from, and even opposite to, that of the public ... The proposal of any new law or regulation of commerce which comes from this order ... ought never to be adopted, till after having been long and carefully examined ... with the most suspicious attention. It comes from an order of men ... who have generally an interest to deceive and even oppress the public" - Adam Smith, Economist

"People don't care how much you know until they know how much you care" - Theodore Roosevelt

CHAPTER 3

THE AMERICAN DREAM &

POLITICAL CORRUPTION

Americans like to think we have a meritocracy where the "American Dream" can be pursued by anyone. Certainly there are dramatic examples of this, but statistically speaking socioeconomic mobility in the US ranks behind Canada, Germany, Australia, France, Italy, and the UK - and the trend is down. In the US in 1973 those born into the bottom socioeconomic quartile had a 23% chance to move into the top socioeconomic quartile, compared to 10% in 1998.

Social scientists use a statistic called income mobility elasticity as an indicator of overall social mobility. Essentially it measures the degree to which rich fathers have rich sons and poor fathers have poor sons. The US ranks worst among our peers while our neighbor Canada ranks best.

Another "rags to riches" measure looks at percent of sons going from the bottom income quartile to the top income quartile. Again the US is at the bottom among peers, and more telling, the rate is in decline, being half what it was 25 years ago.

> A study by the Economic Policy Institute found that from 1979 to 2012, productivity of the average American worker increased nearly 75 percent. The study further found that over that same time span, real income only increased 5 percent. In other words the average worker's productivity rose 15 times more than pay. If the majority is producing more but earning less who is going to buy all those goods? In part those goods were bought with consumer borrowing which led to debt problems and the current "deleveraging". This does not bode well for an economy that is some 70 percent dependent on consumer spending. These factors have led to businesses not investing, sitting on large piles of cash, and waiting for demand to turn around - they are probably in for a long wait.

> Up until the 1980's average corporate CEO total compensation generally topped out at some 40 times the average worker's total compensation. Today we find that average corporate CEO total compensation has risen dramatically to some 200 times the average worker's total compensation, a fivefold increase. Have CEO's become five times more productive than the average worker in that time frame or is something else at work here?

First of all, modern times see much more CEO compensation coming in the form of stock options and bonuses tied to performance. This makes it easier for a corporate board of directors to justify what ultimately proves to be overly rich total compensation packages inclusive of large guaranteed pensions. Secondly, most corporate boards relate with executive management in a "clubby" less than independent atmosphere where other stakeholders are secondary. Critics claim the net result is excessive risk taking and focus on short term results.

"Supply Side Economics", which came into vogue during the 1980's "Reagonomics" years, uses what is called the "Laffer" curve which says that at tax rates of 0% and 100% the government will raise no revenue since 100% is confiscatory and incentives are totally gone. At somewhere between 0% and 100% government maximizes tax revenues and economic growth. The problem is that determining where the "sweet spot" is on the curve is difficult and corrupted by ulterior agendas that make it easy for politicians to lower taxes without reducing spending, thereby creating crippling huge deficits. Is crippling government a viable path to smaller government? History has not been kind to "Supply Side Economics" ideologues. We have essentially had some 30 plus years since Ronald Reagan came into office to prove the concept. In fact average economic growth in that 30 plus years was less than average economic growth in the 30 years before "Reagonomics".

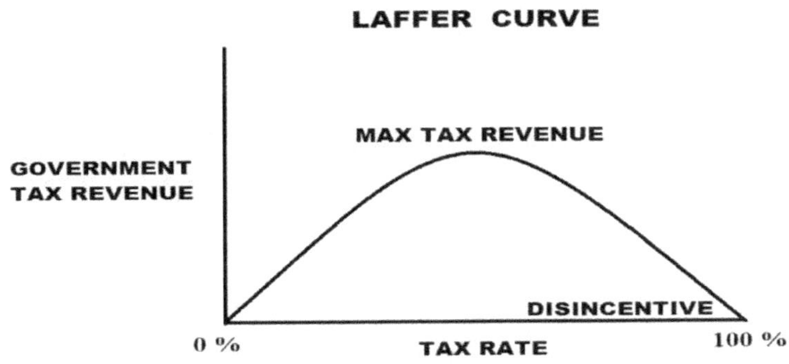

Thirty some years of misguided "Supply Side" policies have contributed to the decline of the middle class and a dramatic concentration of wealth in the US compared to other countries - the top 400 families have the same wealth as the bottom 150 million families. Social scientists have found that societies with more equal distribution of wealth have less of a problem with crime, violence, drug abuse, mental illness, and obesity. Interestingly, just having a higher per capita income does not have the same effect as raw rich/poor gap. But societal costs aside, it is ironic that the wealth concentration that has accompanied "Supply Side" policies has created a demand problem that is hurting economic growth. The last time this same degree of wealth concentration occurred was in 1928, which of course preceded the Great Depression. Juxtaposed to the "Laffer" curve is a new curve I will call the "Laffee" curve. It shows that when 100% of the wealth is held by 1 family there is a demand problem and no economic activity.

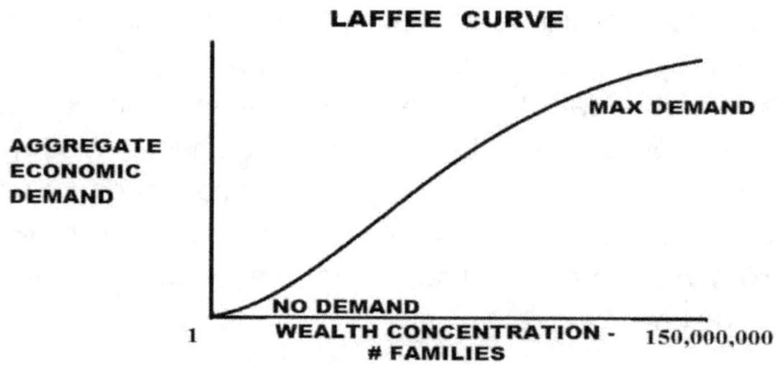

➤ Is any one's time worth $1,000,000 per hour? Apparently so, as in 2013 the top 25 hedge fund managers take home pay was an aggregate 23 billion dollars, with several managers raking in over 2 billion dollars. And by the way, taxpayers subsidized their performance via a very favorable 15% capital gains tax rate.

➤ In 2014 economist and the world's leading expert in income and wealth inequality, Thomas Piketty published his widely read 700 page book Capitalism in the 21st Century. Using extensive data analysis Piketty showed that historically the return on capital has exceeded economic growth, leading to increasing concentrations of wealth by the holders of capital and creating a "patrimonial capitalism" where "rentiers" derive large incomes from inherited wealth rather than effort and talent, i.e., human capital becomes secondary.   More recently this diminution of the importance of human capital comes from subpar economic performance and lots of students with big student debts but no job. **So the picture is one of an economically "neutered" sub class that is also politically "neutered" since wealth concentration tends to be accompanied by a concentration of political power and oligarchy that sustains the status quo for elites.** This has of course created great turmoil in the US among growing the pie bigger, trickle down, supply side ideologues.   Their main rebuttal has been that Piketty did not adequately account for transfer payments such as social security, or wealth effects such as home values.   They are however missing the main point which is that the very idea of an American meritocracy with accompanying social mobility is in jeopardy. **We don't want a conflicted society of servants attending to wealthy patriarchs / oligarchs - we want a non-conflicted society free from poverty that enables all citizens to pursue and achieve their dreams.** Piketty proposes a "global" tax on wealth to alleviate the problem, but this presumes a political environment not controlled by elites. Seriously addressing the wealth concentration problem Thomas Piketty uncovers requires political reform centered in political equality, and that is what this book is all about.

> The Washington DC metro area has the highest median income and the 3 wealthiest counties in the US, but also has the highest rate in the US (>30%) for childhood food insecurity (i.e., poverty). This sounds more "third world" gated community than world super power. Perhaps the political elite culture in Washington is more interested in personal enrichment than public service. To get above the poverty line ($23,050 for a family of four in 2012) earning

federal minimum wage ($7.25 in 2012) requires 2 family wage earners or multiple jobs moonlighting. Children in these families suffer from birth and are likely to never break out of the poverty cycle.

In the US children from single parent female head of household families are more than five times likely to live in poverty than families with two parents. The anti-poverty paradigm is education first, then job, then marriage, then child bearing. The number of single parent families has more than tripled since 1960, and 90 percent of those are female head of household. Fortunately the "War on Poverty", initiated in the 1960's, has helped to drop the odds of a single parent female head of household living in poverty from 50 percent to 34 percent. But this has been swamped by the dramatic increase in the total number of single parent female head of household families.

You can be fairly certain that if corporations had barriers to their success there would be plenty of Congressional public hearings, a bee's nest of lobbying activity, and legislation to address the problems. The some 50,000,000 Americans who make up the "invisible poor" by comparison will get none of that because they have no money. There is little serious dialogue of consequence going on here because of the attitude this is a problem that can be solved magically without government programs by family values and personal responsibility. We need funded government programs that do the following and more:
1. Provide life skills training in schools for teens covering realities of relationships, child rearing, and making a living.
2. Advocate child support enforcement, independent of whether there was a marriage or not.
3. Incentives for employers to make workplace reforms that allow single parents to balance competing demands of work and family.

> They say money corrupts and you will find more of it in Washington DC than anywhere else in America. The Washington DC metro area has the highest median income in the US. Of 3141 counties in the US the top 3 in median income are in the Washington DC metro area (Loudoun, Fairfax, and Arlington). This is of course where our political elites including lobbyists live.

On the surface lobbyists are there to provide information to Congress so that good legislation results. This used to be done to a large degree in open public Congressional hearings. Over the years however the number of public hearings has declined and has been replaced by backroom deals between lobbyists seeking favors and legislators seeking money for reelection campaigns. Studies show a typical legislator now spends most of their time fund raising because a preponderance of elections are won by the candidate spending the most money. Even more corrupting is the fact (2000-2004 data) that about half of former members of Congress go on to be lobbyists with $1,000,000 plus annual compensation packages. Former Congressional staffers who become lobbyists can expect $300,000 plus annual compensation packages. Perversely, these staffers serve as gatekeepers to Congressional access and spend their time getting cozy with lobbyists rather that dealing with constituents.

This all creates a myopic insular self-serving feeding frenzy that seems to do well irrespective of the rest of the country. From 1983 to 2009, even adjusted for inflation, expenditures on lobby activity increased by some 700% as the number of registered lobby organizations more than doubled. Approximately half of those lobby organizations represent business and about half of business lobbying is to get tax breaks, resulting in that same time span a tripling of our tax code to 66,000 pages. The other half of business lobbying is to get "rules" that are in their favor and therefore contribute to crony capitalism. But this is all supposedly free speech and not at all indicative of political inequality - is a culture of self-serving greed much better than a culture of public service for the common good? Has the lobbied political culture shifted dramatically away from dreaming of an interstate highway system benefitting all towards scheming of a bridge to nowhere serving few?

➤ The Supreme Court's Citizens United decision has opened the money'd flood gates on political inequality. In the 2012 elections 28 percent of the 6 billion dollars in political contributions came from the top 1% of the top 1% wealthy elites (1 in 10,000). According to Sunlight Foundation, most wealthy elites are associated with corporations. Even more telling is the concentrated spending on key Congressional leaders. In recent past elections House minority leader Nancy Pelosi received 40 percent of her funds from wealthy elites. House majority leader Eric Cantor received 34 percent of his funds from wealthy elites. Speaker of the House John Boehner received 32 percent of his funds from wealthy elites. All this money is a windfall to our "watchdog" media, to the extent they become coopted to big money in politics under the guise of "free speech" (i.e., our watchdog media has become a lapdog to big money).

➤ Knee jerk liberals, and conservatives for that matter, should sit on their hands while reading what follows. We should consider eliminating the corporate income tax along with rewriting our convoluted bloated rocket science tax code. Firstly, even though the US's published corporate income tax rate of 35% is higher than most of the rest of the world, the actual rate typically runs less than 15% because of corporate money's lobbying clout. The corporate income tax is actually a small and growing even smaller source of revenue. Instead of giving highly preferential tax rates to capital gains and dividends because of the double taxation on corporate profits argument, we should tax those more like ordinary income and thereby more than make up for lost corporate income tax revenue. Why should capital, currently controlled primarily by the ultra- wealthy, be so highly tax favored over worker income, especially when we are awash in capital that sits idle because a shrinking middle class has stifled economic demand? Secondly, because large international corporations hold some 2 trillion dollars offshore to avoid US taxes, we would invite some of this money home where it could be used in investments creating jobs. Thirdly, since perhaps half of the money spent on lobbying and reelection campaigns comes from corporations trying to game the tax code, we would eliminate a large source of corrupting influence. But therein lies the problem. Political elites, lobbyists and politicians alike, will be reluctant to give up this lever on their cash machine. They will come up with good sounding straw man arguments such as what's to keep individual's masquerading as corporations to get the zero rate (the IRS already police's such activity). But hang in there. This is one where sticking the big bad corporations is flawed thinking. Rather this is a back door ethics and corruption reform that drains some of the money out of bad politics.

Few in America would argue that a society with little social mobility is a good thing, especially if that society is delusional in thinking it is the ultimate meritocracy where the American Dream is alive for all. Lack of social mobility, coupled with a growing gap between the rich and poor, leads to societal costs, such as lower health outcomes and higher crime. Talk of "growing the pie bigger" and "taking responsibility" means little if not accompanied by a healthy environment of social mobility. Social mobility will suffer as long as there is political inequality and two sets of rules. Two sets of rules mean less justice and liberty for those not represented in making the rules.   The bottom line is our governmental system is failing us badly and we need to change it.

➢ Americans are perhaps most proud of and protective of their freedom. From the pilgrims on, freedom of religion was and continues to be very important. To maintain religious freedom we separate church and state. We don't want any particular religious group to meddle in government and use it as a tool to further its particular beliefs. Similarly, religious groups do not want government meddling in their beliefs as long as those beliefs do not infringe on freedom in general and the common good.

With this in mind one might ask, if we value free markets to any degree, why would we not strive to separate large corporations and state? I think the answer to that is that large corporations, unlike religious groups, have a history of infringing on freedom in general and the common good. So we have antitrust laws and regulation to curb this. Currently, however, this has been "turned upside down" as large corporations, with lots of money to lobby with, often view government as a tool to be gamed and used to their advantage. Unequal "free speech" tied to access and money creates a corrupt crony capitalist system. Since the political elites benefit from this they protect the status quo and it is difficult to change. This is a long journey, and it starts by committing over an extended time to total political equality. But this is our history - starting with giving blacks, then women, the right to vote, and proceeding now to political equality and having those votes actually count for something.

➢ **There are major choke points in our democratic systems that prevent your vote from actually counting for something. The first choke point is the "money election" held before all elections, where aspiring candidates raising the most money** from big money special interests are preselected to go on and become actual candidates. The second choke point is winner take all Democrat versus Republican voting. The third choke point is voting every two year election cycle and hoping there is something in a party platform that actually happens between elections. The fourth choke point is your limited access between elections as opposed to money'd access which is ongoing. The fifth choke point is Congressional games and rules that whip your representative into strictly partisan mode.

The Swiss system of "direct democracy" has no such choke points. Swiss direct democracy has been evolving for some 800 plus years. The Swiss are very proud of their democratic system which is among the least corrupt in the world. Why? The main reason is Swiss direct democracy is a two way street via citizen / voter referendums and initiatives. If big money wanted to game the system and get special rules, the money would have to be spread over most of the citizenry, not just a few chokepoint representatives. The Swiss "return on government" has made them among the world leaders in global economic competitiveness and growth, per capita income, low unemployment, and budgetary balance.

"Men fear thought as they fear nothing else on earth -- more than ruin, more even than death. Thought is subversive and revolutionary, destructive and terrible, thought is merciless to privilege, established institutions, and comfortable habits; thought is anarchic and lawless, indifferent to authority, careless of the well-tried wisdom of the ages. Thought looks into the pit of hell and is not afraid ... Thought is great and swift and free, the light of the world, and the chief glory of man." - Bertrand Russell, Philosopher, Political Activist

CHAPTER 4

GOVERNMENT OF UNEQUAL REPRESENTATION

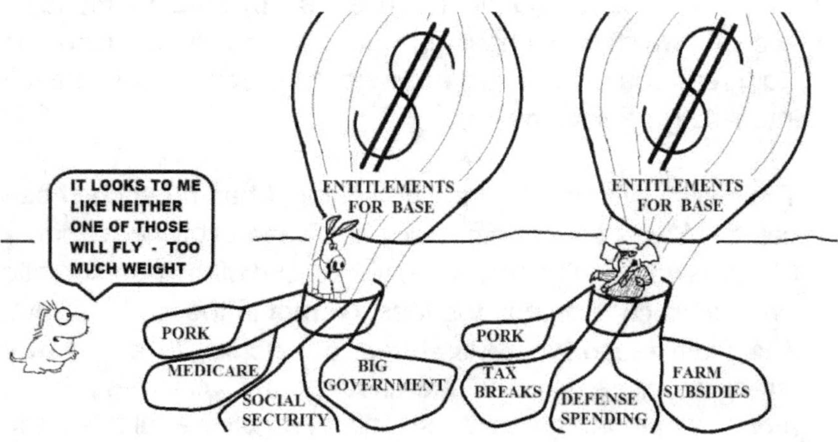

Some 200 plus years ago when American representative democracy was set up most people were tied to the land, rarely ventured from home, and communicated at the speed of a horse. Because of this any form of democracy required that it be carried out by representatives, primarily prominent white men of wealth, who had the ability to devote themselves to politics. The reliance on political elites soon led to major problems with political inequality and corruption. The civil war, women's suffrage, civil rights movement, and more currently Occupy Wall Street and Tea Party interests are examples of battles with the political elite and political inequality.

> ➢ Gerrymandering is the practice of politicians selecting voters rather than voters selecting politicians. Gerrymandering, done at the state level, explains in part why a political party can win a plurality of House of Representative seats in a given state while faring much worse in the statewide popular vote. For example in the 2000 election the swing states of

Florida, Pennsylvania, Ohio, and Michigan split 50/50 on the presidential vote while the Republicans won 51 House seats to the Democrats 26, a margin of nearly 2 to 1. In the 2012 election estimates are that the Democrats would have to get 55% of the popular vote nationwide to win the House. This of course translates into political inequality. Congressional districts are mapped by state legislatures on a mostly partisan basis and usually in response to the US census every 10 years. The process of gerrymandering involves "packing" and "cracking" voting geographies until you get a maximum of voting districts likely to vote your way. This starts at the state level, where in the 2016 elections some 40 percent of voting districts for state representative had a ballot listing only the incumbent - i.e. potential challengers knew they did not have a chance from the get-go and did not run. The bottom line is that political elites institutionalize political inequality to remain in power. Gerrymandering is only one tool of "voter suppression".

➤ The US Constitution states the House of Representatives will choose a Speaker, who need not be an elected member of Congress. In practice the Speaker of the House of Representatives is an elected member of the House and comes from the majority party. The Speaker of the House controls the House Rules Committee, and thereby exerts dictatorial control over what legislation gets "brought to the floor" for vote. Legislation that the Speaker does not like can be "bottled up in committee" and not brought to the floor for a vote. Legislation that the Speaker does like can be "dumped to the floor" for a vote with instructions not to debate or amend. Is this not a major source of gridlock, or at the other extreme non deliberation? What is the point of electing a Representative if that Representative is routinely denied the right to vote, or at the other extreme instructed how to vote? Is there not a need for a "check and balance" here?

Part and parcel to political inequality is corruption. On its surface lobbying activity is useful in presenting lawmakers with useful views and information. In practice when it is linked to money for election campaigns, or potential future lucrative lobbyist jobs, it is insidiously corrupt. **We end up with two sets of rules and a small number of winners, the rest of us all being relative losers. To appease the masses and remain in control both political parties overspend or under tax and build entitlement and debt levels that are unsustainable – we decline as a nation.**

> During the economic collapse that was the Depression Congress passed the Glass Steagall Act which limited the high risk investment activities of commercial banks. The rationale was that a stable commercial banking system making routine loans was vital for a healthy economy, and high risk banking activities were a major factor causing the Depression.

Starting in the 1970's corporate competition on steroids started spilling over into lobbying activity in Washington DC, turning "K Street" into "Gucci Gulch" as the money poured in. Ex politicians and ex political staffers started taking lucrative lobbying careers at 10 times former salaries. Lobbying gradually eroded the provisions of the Glass Steagall Act culminating in 1999 when the Glass Steagall Act was repealed under pretexts certain banks had to be made more globally competitive, and banks in general had to be able to be "supermarkets" of financial services to better serve their customers and diversify their sources of revenue, thereby becoming even more stable.

The role of Glass Steagall repeal in causing the "Great Recession" is much debated. Obviously political elites who were coopted by insidious money'd lobbying activity minimize the role of Glass Steagall repeal in near financial collapse. On the other side of the debate critics contend that Glass

Steagall repeal was the final tipping point in a growing culture of banking system risk appetite and loose regulation. Critics also state global competitiveness and "financial supermarket" aside, the real driver of all this was multimillion dollar "star" executive compensation and bonus packages that created a gambling casino culture of greed with the tax payer ultimately on the hook. Critics also contend that what the country really needs is a staid humdrum loan making banking utility that even a monkey could run by taking low cost money from the federal reserve, marking it up a few percentage points, and loaning it out to entities that can reasonably be expected to pay it back (as in Canada, which did not have the problems the US had during the financial crisis).

➤ New York City vies with London to be the top international financial center. The stakes are high, involving trillions of dollars in client accounts. High on the list of "supermarket global services" is management of offshore accounts set up to avoid taxes by rich corporations and individuals, including leading political figures. The global pervasiveness of offshore tax avoidance by money'd entities is just now coming to the general public's attention. In the US the Government Accounting Office (GAO) recently found that 83% of the largest corporations and 63% of the government's largest contractors used offshore tax havens. A 2008 US Senate report estimates the US loses some 100 billion dollars a year in tax revenue due to offshore tax havens. There is major irony in all of this.

The first major source of irony is the financial services industry lobbying government to loosen regulations so they could be more globally competitive and offer a "supermarket of services", when a large part of those services is "offshoring" to help clients avoid paying taxes to the same government being lobbied. The second major source of irony is corporations, and the wealthy that "offshore", having disproportionate sway with our elected representatives through their big money lobby and election funding activities. Is this not Boston Tea Party back asswards "representation without taxation"? Should entities that set up "offshore tax residences" in foreign countries to escape taxes, be considered resident citizens by the Supreme Court, and therefore able to spend endless "free speech" money to dominate our politics?

➢ "Private Equity" is one offering in the financial services industry's "supermarket of services". The term "Private Equity" is actually a euphemistic "rebranding" of the 1980's era term "Leveraged Buyout". The 1980's saw corporate raiders targeting companies they could take over, strip assets, and load up with debt to bolster their own "takeout" personal fortunes before divesting and moving on to the next target. The game turns tragic when the overleveraged target companies can no longer meet debt obligations and go bankrupt. In the 1980's this also resulted in the bankruptcy of financial services firm Drexel Burnham & Lambert, along with felony charges. The other part of the story is the disruption caused in the lives of all the targeted company employees that lost their jobs. Efficient allocation of capital is an essential part of capitalism, so "private equity" is evil to the degree it is driven to the extreme by greed.

➢ POGO, or Project on Government Oversight, is a nonprofit government watchdog that has documented how a "revolving door" of government regulators, going to and from high paying jobs at private companies they regulate corrupts good regulation that is in the public's interest. This is of course in addition to the corruption caused by big money'd special interests lobbying Congress. This is a difficult and pernicious problem since regulation often creates winners and losers. The winners of course like regulation because it often reduces competition and is a barrier to entry by competitors. Coopted government regulation contributes to crony capitalism, less than free markets, and slow economic and job growth.

This is also a large source of political hypocrisy where the walk does not match the talk. Politicians will talk about not liking regulations which stifle the economy and job creation, while at the same time taking big money for their reelections from lobbyists pushing regulations not necessarily in the public's interest. Ultimately the solution to this is to replace cozy back room deals with more open public comment and review along with reducing the influence of money'd lobbyists with politicians. **Over the long run an environment and culture of political equality will greatly reduce what has become two sets of rules.**

To gain and retain political power the Democrats back social welfare programs such as Medicare and Social Security for their political base. Less talked about but just as problematic are Republican's backing of defense spending, farm subsidies, privatization contracts, and "wealthfare" tax cuts / breaks for crony capitalist oligarchs. Medicare, Social Security, and Defense spending each consistently run more than 20% of federal spending, dwarfing all other expense categories. The US spends more on defense than all of the rest of the world combined. Both Democrats and Republicans have been guilty of earmarks (which allow lawmakers to add language to bills ordering a federal agency to spend a specific amount on a project back home) and need only look to their congressional leaders who have remained in office for a long time due to their mastery of pork. Congress has become a bastion of hypocrisy and delusion.

➢ In 2010 the House of Representatives banned earmarks with the Senate following suit in 2011. This forced lawmakers into less direct methods of obtaining pork. Following the 2016 presidential election lawmakers, citing gridlock, have shown great interest in bringing the earmark process back. **In the bigger picture this is a battle as to whether we want to put our faith in a government that depends on having a sound system of government in place, or a government that depends on ad hoc deal making to work around the gross inadequacies of a non-working governmental system. Deal making favors the current wasteful and ineffective status quo of government.**

➢ You may or may not remember the infamous Alaskan "bridge to nowhere" - a 398 million dollar bridge earmark proposed by Republicans in Alaska to reach an island with 50 residents. In 2007 Alaska ranked 1st with **+ $7448** per capita net gain in dollars (taxation-spending) received from Washington. Delaware ranked last with - $12,285 per capita net loss in dollars sent to Washington. Political inequality translates into "net dollar flow" winners and losers among states rank ordered as follows:

Winners: Alaska, New Mexico, Mississippi, Virginia, West Virginia, Alabama, Hawaii, North Dakota, South Dakota, Maine

Losers: Delaware, Minnesota, New Jersey, Connecticut, New York, Illinois, Nebraska, Rhode Island, Texas, Colorado

These relationships have proved consistent over time. Winners were generally more rural "Red" or Republican states. Losers were generally more urban "Blue" or Democratic states. A 2015 analysis by personal finance website WalletHub used 3 metrics to look at state dependence on the Federal government. The metrics were

Federal dollar inflows per every dollar paid in Federal income tax, percent of state funding coming from the Federal government, and the number of Federal employees per capita. The analysis concluded that Republican leaning states tended to be more dependent on the Federal government than Democrat leaning states. When we think of "entitlements" we tend to think of Democrats and Social Security and Medicare. The numbers show Republicans have their own entitlements consisting of tax loopholes, defense spending, farm subsidies, and Congressional pork/earmarks.

The big question here is if Republicans are the party of small government, entitlement reform, and free markets, as opposed to "crony" capitalism, why do the "Red" rural states fare so well in getting government largesse? Is this not tending to the base? Is this not doing the talk but not the walk hypocrisy?

The biggest hypocrisy is that your congress person represents you. There are 435 members in the House of Representatives, which means each represents about 750,000 citizens. Assuming a normal work week and the representative does nothing but talk to constituents, you get about 10 seconds of your representative's time each year - 20 seconds if you consider supporters of the opposing party will get 0 seconds.

No problem - we have large and ever growing congressional staffs to help serve constituents. Using the most recent number of an average of 14 staff members per representative gets you up to 280 seconds per year. In fact if you have ever tried to contact a representative you get the distinct impression that the staff act not as public servants but as gatekeepers to "keep you off" their boss. The best you can hope for is a canned mail response. You may get a phone call if you have donated to their campaign and might do so in the future, or if there is potential for either good or bad publicity. The big money gets direct access using a lobbyist that knows how to play the game. The Senate is similar to the House with a few twists.

> ➤ Not counting the staff of the Congressional Research Service, the Congressional Budget Office, and the General Accounting Office, there are currently some 14,000 Congressional Staffers with annual costs closing in on 1 billion dollars. But those costs pale in comparison to the costs associated with coopted legislation resulting from legislative access and lobbying tainted by money. Legistorm, a nonpartisan group, finds that nearly 5400 current and former congressional staffers have been through the "lobbying revolving door" in the past decade alone. Some 600 former lobbyists now sit on Congressional Staffs. There is a cozy back room atmosphere here created by the prospects of $300,000 plus annual lobbyist salaries. Perhaps part of government reform should be a reduction in Congressional staffing levels. We're not seeing a return on all this staffing, and it primarily feeds the insular elitist money'd culture of Washington.

> ➤ **Jack Abramoff is a former Washington DC lobbyist who along with 21 others was convicted in 2006 of conspiracy to bribe public officials, along with tax evasion. In a subsequent memoir he wrote that the best way for lobbyists to influence people in DC is to casually suggest they join their lobbying firm after "public service" . . . "the moment I said that to them or any of our staff said that to them, that was it, we owned them." One could call this preemptive bribery, and it's the air DC breathes. Solving this corruption problem is a long term project involving major culture change.**

> ➤ It is against the law for politicians to divert political contributions towards personal use - this is of course bribery.

When that law was created however, the "Leadership PAC" was also created as a loophole personal political expense account, typically funded by lobbyists and special interest groups to curry favor. Most Congressmen have a Leadership PAC, and typical abuses include paying personal expenses and putting family members on the payroll. At the extreme, a former Presidential hopeful used Leadership PAC funds to pay his mistress $114,000 to do a campaign video.

> Political corruption is widespread and legal in the context of loopholes provisioned by the political elite. One approach to fixing our corrupt dysfunctional government is to take big money out of the picture. Trevor Potter, former chairman of the Federal Elections Commission, or FEC, is seeking to build public support for the "American Anti-Corruption Act". This Act essentially curtails big money lobby activity and influence. I fully support this effort, though it is far from a sure thing since it faces major hurdles. The first major hurdle is taking the controlling political elite head on and threatening their cash machine. The second hurdle is the Supreme Court which has considered big money part of free speech. The final hurdle is history, which shows the ability of the political elite to constantly circumvent the rules via loopholes. **We really need to change the entire dynamics, culture, and "personality" of our representative democracy, and in the chapters that follow I propose a means to do just that.**

CHAPTER 5

GOVERNMENT OF NON DELIBERATION

The primary focus of the House of Representatives was, and is, as the name implies, representing citizen constituents. A shorter 2 year election cycle along with fewer constituents implicitly made House members more responsive to day to day issues of the American populace. The primary focus of the Senate was, and is, deliberating issues that are more long term and strategic in nature. The longer 6 year term and fewer members were supposed to enable this. Until the 17th amendment in 1912, Senators were not popularly elected, but rather were elected by state legislatures.

> ➢ When our government's election processes were first set up the rationale for having state legislatures elect US Senators was that this was somewhat the way the Continental Congress had been set up, plus state legislators would know the candidates better than the general populace. There was a general distrust of the general populace, especially since colonists loyal to King George were still out there.   This

system however was prone to backroom corruption including numerous instances (9) of outright bribery. Also numerous were instances (45) where squabbling, gridlocked state legislatures failed to elect any Senator at all, sometimes for as long as 4 years. Are these problems not endemic to representative government in general?

Rather than forego having a US Senator, state legislatures starting letting direct popular vote decide until some 29 states used popular vote and thereby "forced" the passing of the 17th amendment to elect Senators by popular vote. Processes to amend the constitution, aside from 1789 when the 10 amendments of the Bill of Rights were passed, has over the years allowed only 17 of some 10,000 potential amendments to pass, leaving us with such obvious faults as still using the electoral college rather than popular vote to pick the President, and having Washington DC without any voting representation in Congress. Maintenance is an important fact of life. When we hear our car making an ominous noise we are putting our family at risk if we let it go, and wait for something to break. That is precisely what we are doing with constitutional amendment processes overly skewed towards great difficulty.

➢ A vote for President in Wyoming counts about 3X as much as a vote for President in California. This is because we still use the Electoral College and not popular vote to choose the President. Wyoming gets three votes in the Electoral College because it has one member in the House and two members in the Senate. The same 3X leverage applies to six other states.   Historically there have been five presidential elections where the winner in the Electoral College, which counts, did not win the popular vote, which doesn't count. Four of these elections went Republican while another went Whig, which was a forerunner to the Republican Party. **So the way our governmental system was set up some 200 plus**

years ago has major institutional political inequalities (up to 3X) built into it.

> There is a reason why states with small populations such as Alaska do so well in net dollars to/from Washington. Alaska has three Congressional votes to use in trading votes for "deals", which is about 3 times the trading power of California per capita. When "the whip" comes around looking for votes small population states can and do bury proportionately more pork in legislative bills. Major spending bills often run more than 1000 pages – to the point few read them in their entirety and know what is in them. This of course all helps with reelection, so Congressional leaders who have been around for a while decry pork publicly, while at the same embracing and mastering it.

The cost of pork, and earmarks, is only part of the picture to the extent pork takes money away from more pressing national priorities. For example the Army decided it did not need to spend 436 million dollars on the Abrams tank – that there were other more pressing needs. Congressmen representing constituencies where the Abrams tank was made prevailed and saved the Abrams. Since these Congressmen were "big defense supporters" and "deficit hawks" the hypocrisy ran deep.

The House of Representatives has too few members to adequately do its mission of representing citizens. The founding fathers perhaps did not see us moving to a nation of more than 300 million citizens. In contrast the Senate has too many members to adequately do its mission of deliberating strategic long term issues. The founding fathers perhaps did not see us moving from 13 to 50 states. The size of a deliberative group is one of the most important factors in effectiveness. Too large and there are not enough opportunities for effective communication among members. Too small and there is not enough breadth of experience and viewpoints to get the whole picture, as when you effectively have only two opposing viewpoints, Democratic and Republican.

The Senate has tried to address the "too many" problem by breaking up into some 20 committees and 68 sub-committees. The leadership of the two parties decides who is assigned to which committee / sub-committee and this is a major cause of bipartisan gridlock - i.e., buck the party line and your coveted "plum" committee assignment is in jeopardy or your committee work will never make it to the full Senate floor for consideration. The too many problem reverts to a too few problem since viewpoints differing from the two party lines are stifled. Purposeful deliberation in the Senate becomes nonexistent because party leadership prevents bills from going to the full Senate floor. Bills that are "dumped" to the floor are too big to be fully read, or debated in any meaningful way and come with implied instructions by the majority party leadership not to debate, or amend, but pass. But most Senators don't care because their vote has been secured beforehand by party leadership burying pork in the bill. Faced with this scenario, the opposing party may "filibuster" which in days gone by meant actual marathon talking on the Senate floor, but in modern times means just stating your intent to filibuster. **The bottom line is we get bills loaded up like Christmas trees that aggravate government deficits, or gridlock where nothing gets done on major problems facing us.**

> The Senate is a place of front room theater and backroom deals. First in the tools of front room theater, and non-debate, is the filibuster as made famous by Jimmy Stewart in the movie Mr. Smith Goes to Washington. Filibusters are a procedural Senate maneuver used by outnumbered lawmakers to try to sidetrack a legislative bill. It used to require a marathon of speeches requiring the opposition to get cots and keep a majority of votes nearby in case the

speeches ended and a vote gets called for. Now all it requires is that the outnumbered lawmakers inform the Senate that 60 of 100 votes will be required to pass a bill. In 1939 when Jimmy Stewart made the movie there were no filibusters. Recently they have averaged more than 40 per year - ample evidence of partisan gridlock.

Jimmy Stewart prevailed in the movie, bolstered by an outpouring of public support. But powerful money'd lobbying can, and does trump public support as was seen in 2013 when driven by the Newtown Connecticut killings at an elementary school, some 90% of the public supported expanded background checks before guns are sold, but no action was taken even on a watered down bill. At the other extreme, and perhaps most disturbing to libertarian types, was the Patriot Act following 911 which basically approved a wish list of surveillance activities by government agencies which infringed on Constitutional Rights. There was overwhelming popular support and the Patriot Act was rammed through Congress by congressional leaders in short order by bypassing normal committee constitutional expertise and hearings, and put to vote with the understanding there would be minimal debate and no amendments. Ironically, the US has seven times the per capita deaths from gun violence than neighboring Canada, and deaths from gun violence in the US since and including "911", have outnumbered deaths from terrorism by a factor approaching 50 to 1. The bottom line is Senate leaders and Senate rules and procedures make it much less than a center of honest debate our founding fathers wanted. They have made it rather a conduit for both errors of omission such as Newtown gun control, and errors of commission such as parts of the Patriot Act.

➤ A party whip, as the name implies, uses punishments or inducements to keep party members from wandering too far from the aims of party leadership. Party members who do stray too far may limit their committee assignments and pork / earmark opportunities. This of course stifles debate and enforces gridlock and control by a few party leaders via back room deals. The question arises, what does the typical American accomplish by actually listening and understanding a political candidate's positions every 2 or 6 years when this means nothing in a system controlled by a few party leaders and their whips? Is this not an outmoded feudal system with an oath of fealty to a particular party's select few leaders along with incessant warfare? Are not the shrinking middle class, and growing ranks of poor, serfs in a new "neo feudalism", with a central government put on a path to ineffective non-relevance done purposely by small government ideologues pushing trillion dollar deficits?

The most recent attempt to fix Congress has been the use of super committees such as Simpson-Bowles, whose members are typically former members of Congress representing both parties. On the plus side these super committees try to inject a balanced senior statesman, above the fray, long term strategic approach to problems. On the minus side, this approach has not worked because in "not invented here fashion", it lacks widespread public input and support, and does not come with voting clout in either the House or Senate.

➤ The committee / sub-committee system Congress uses is highly partisan and controlled by party leaders that control who gets on what committee. In hopes of getting beyond gridlock, presidents have set up bipartisan "Commissions" of senior statesman types. Since 1990 there have been 13 of these Commissions. The most recent of these is the "Simpson Bowles Super Committee", named after former Republican Senator Alan Simpson and former Democratic Senator Erskine Bowles. This Super Committee came up with a bipartisan framework to solve our fiscal and deficit problems, but their work, which included Social Security and Medicare reforms, went nowhere. The Simpson Bowles framework went nowhere for two reasons. First of all the Super Committee did not have voting privileges in Congress beyond the usual "whipped partisan gridlocked" votes. Secondly, the appointed Super Committee did not come with significant "political capital" of the type that comes from voting support by the general public. It was easy for House and Senate leaders to ignore it and not bring it to a vote.

But let's look at what the "Simpson Bowles Super Committee" really represents. It represents an attempt by our government to address major looming problems by looking at a longer term strategic direction beyond flip flopping every 2 or 4 year election cycle. Successful modern organizations do this strategic view and planning with the help of a standing Board of Directors elected by stakeholders - not unlike a Super Committee but with more independence and clout. Successful modern organizations also realize that the Executive job and function, especially for large global organizations, is perhaps too big for one person, and therefore a Board of Directors is a valuable resource to the degree that it has diverse and experienced senior statesmen. In 1776 there was no such thing as a Board of Directors. In modern times every successful organization has a Board of Directors except our federal government. This Board of Directors function will never come from the dysfunctional House or Senate. Rather, it will come from an extension and modification of the Commission / Super Committee concept as I will present later.

There is major irony and hypocrisy in all this since this dysfunctional and corrupt system creates major winners and losers. The big winners are political elite career politicians and lobbyists. In public they decry the way things are working, but beneath the surface they are remiss to change a system that does nothing other than maintain the status quo fueled by money for reelection. The other major winners are of course those with lots of money for lobbying activity. The major losers have been the middle class and the poor. Over the long run there are no winners because the system becomes so irrationally out of balance, with false expectations pushed by the two parties to stay in power. The Republicans push "a bigger pie" via free market capitalism which is an economic impossibility in an environment of political inequality where the rules pushed by lobbyists create an uneven playing field for business. **Milton Friedman himself said economic freedom can only occur when economic power is separated from political power (i.e. $$$).** When over time the bigger pie does not get shared, there is collapse. The Democrats push false expectations that entitlements are financially sustainable without major adjustments, even though they are a risk to our future as a nation.

We have a political system that is outdated, fails to address major problems, and serves primarily the needs of the political elite. Our nation's standing in the world is at risk. Our social and economic well-being is on a downward trend with no end in sight. **As we enter the promising Internet Age with human and collaborative knowledge and understanding at the highest levels of all time, what can we do to advance democratic processes and society?**

> During the 2012 US presidential campaign Republican candidate Mitt Romney gave what has infamously been called his 47% speech at a private $50,000 per plate fundraiser. A bartender at the event unobtrusively recorded video of the speech on his cell phone camera. In the speech Romney derided what he said were the 47% of Americans who pay no income tax, and in fact participate in a culture of entitlement pandered to by the Democrats. "My job is not to worry about those people. I'll never convince them they should take personal responsibility and care for their lives." To make a long story short the video made its way to the internet and was a big factor in Romney's loss. This is a

"Never doubt that a small group of thoughtful, committed, citizens can change the world. Indeed, it is the only thing that ever has."
- Margaret Mead, Anthropologist

"A human being is a part of the whole called by us universe, a part limited in time and space. He experiences himself, his thoughts and feeling as something separated from the rest, a kind of optical delusion of his consciousness. This delusion is a kind of prison for us, restricting us to our personal desires and to affection for a few persons nearest to us. Our task must be to free ourselves from this prison by widening our circle of compassion to embrace all living creatures and the whole of nature in its beauty." - Albert Einstein

"We had to struggle with the old enemies of peace - business and financial monopoly, speculation, reckless banking, class antagonism, sectionalism, war profiteering. They had begun to consider the Government of the United States as a mere appendage to their own affairs. We know now that Government by organized money is just as dangerous as Government by organized mob." - Franklin D. Roosevelt

CHAPTER 6

FEDERAL BUREAUCRACY-

EFFICIENCY vs EFFECTIVENESS

Once the executive, legislative, or judicial branch of government makes a policy decision, the federal bureaucracy, with more than 2 million employees, takes over to implement it. The president exercises control over the federal bureaucracy by appointing the right people to head the various agencies, issuing executive orders, altering agency budgets, and reorganizing agencies. Congress exercises control over the federal bureaucracy by influencing the appointment of agency heads, altering agency budgets, holding hearings, and rewriting legislation to make it more detailed, or explicit. **"Control" implies the ability to weaken an agency, and make it ineffective and/or inefficient. This is mainly done by restricting budgets, appointing less than competent agency leadership, or delaying for extended periods, the confirmation of agency leadership.** Lobbyists also lobby the federal bureaucracy, and in fact if they don't hold sway when actual legislation is passed by Congress, they have an ample second chance lobbying the federal bureaucracy.

> A major source of corruption in government is appointment to positions in the bureaucracy. When these appointments are mostly based on party loyalty and not subjected to an approval process they act much like a slush fund for political cronyism where appointees are rewarded with lavish salaries irrespective of competencies and position rigor. Moreover there is often the potential for integrity compromising political contributions and lucrative post service lobbying, consulting, or executive positions in the sector the government bureaucracy deals with.

> Executive orders coming from the President have the full force of law and are reviewable by the Supreme Court. Executive orders are numbered and typically cite an existing law that is being clarified or furthered by the executive order. The Supreme Court has rarely overturned executive orders, and does so only when an executive order is deemed to be making law rather than clarifying or furthering an existing law. If Congress takes issue with an executive order, the recourse is typically an attempt not to fund the part of the law affected by the executive order. In general, partisan battles between Congress and the President become battles over funding or not funding. In this environment government deficits become an excuse and tool for not funding. **Thus to address deficits over the long term, we are not just talking about adjustments in spending and taxes, but rather a fundamental change in the partisan political culture of Washington. In the following chapters of this book a means of changing the partisan political culture, and "personality", of government is presented.**

Each election cycle sees the winning political party try to exercise control over the federal bureaucracy and see that their policies are carried out. There is typically a "honeymoon" period after which agency and lobbying activity tend to "push back" against possible changes and budget cuts. This of course adversely affects exploding federal deficits. The only way around agency and lobby pushback thus far has been budget sequestering and automatic across-the-board budget cuts. This of course is missed opportunity to make government more effective and efficient by reallocating resources to fit priorities. The "revolving door" of bureaucrats turned lobbyists is a corruption problem that persists despite laws promoting more transparency and disclosure. The political elite like the pervasiveness of lobbying because it gives them the opportunity to deal and benefit financially from the system. All of this would be less problematic if we had less partisan gridlock, worked with a shared sense of priorities, and had a goal driven strategic direction originating directly from citizen voters.

> ➢ Military spending is one of the largest items in the US annual budget at over 20% of the total. The annual US military budget is more than all the rest of the world's military budgets combined. A 2014 Wall Street Journal / NBC poll showed 69% of Americans had a great deal of confidence in the military versus only 16% in the federal government and 13% in large corporations. **Most citizens would say the US military is efficient. Efficiency is defined as competency in performance. Since the military is part of government, it follows that government can be efficient also. An efficient military comes from a long term focus, supported by what some would say is more than adequate funding. The focus derives mostly from unwavering Republican fervor paired with quiescent Democrats not inclined to bicker on military issues. In logical manner, it follows that juxtaposed to this is inefficient government, which is created by lack of focus**

deriving from constant partisan bickering and even sabotage manifested in inadequate funding.

Practitioners of management science make a big distinction between efficiency and effectiveness. Efficiency relates to doing something well. Effectiveness relates to making good decisions and doing the right things. One can be very efficient at doing the wrong things. Effectiveness trumps efficiency from the standpoint it is better to be doing the right thing inefficiently than to be doing the wrong thing efficiently. From a military standpoint most US citizens would say engaging in the second Iraq war was the wrong thing to do, and therefore ineffective. Government effectiveness is threatened by money'd special interests and their cozy relationships with political elites. Privatization for the sake of perceived efficiencies, are likely to come at the expense of effectiveness compromised by what amounts to corrupted government.

> The Minerals Management Service, or MMS, is an agency of the US Department of Interior charged with leasing out onshore and offshore sites for exploitation by oil and gas companies. Collections of oil and gas lease royalties amount to tens of billions of dollars per year - a source of US government revenue second only to that of taxes. The Lakewood Colorado branch of MMS operated like a quasi-business, collecting royalties, not in cash but in oil and gas subsequently sold on the open market. In 2009 it was shut down because of years of corruption involving lost revenues, bribes, gifts, expensive junkets, sex, booze, and drugs. On the other side of these transgressions were some very large oil and gas companies. In fact since its inception in 1982, the MMS had a flawed royalty collection system that was basically an honor system, and this was exploited by special interests to avoid paying billions of dollars in royalties.

There is a very important lesson from all of this. The question of small versus big government is trumped by the need for good government, small or big. Running the country with an overall view and culture that most government is bad and small government is good presumes nothing will be done to make government better. Instead government will be eviscerated or "privatized" and we have a self-fulfilling prophecy of failed government.

Perceived "efficiencies" from getting government out of the way or privatizing ignores the larger question of "effectiveness" - i.e., is government doing the right things as in collecting royalties. The first best situation is an effective and efficient government. The second best situation is an effective government that is not so efficient but committed to improving efficiency. The MMS situation ranks below these in desirability since the government is doing the right thing in collecting royalties, but doing it inefficiently with attempts to improve bogged down by the political power of special interests. There is also an attitude by small government ideologues that most government is bad, so inefficiency on the part of government is tolerated for headline value because it is a route to small government, and in circular logic supports the initial distorted world view.

➤ In 1962 President Kennedy made his famous "go to the moon" speech where he pledged the USA would land a man on the moon and return before the end of the decade. At the time we were in a cold war space race with the Soviet Union, and we were losing the race. The USA accomplished this very ambitious goal in 1969. One cannot question the efficiency of this daunting effort. One might debate the effectiveness of committing all these resources to simply going to the moon and back. The effort however, did bolster a burgeoning generation of scientists and engineers, as well as numerous space related enterprises. **The point is** government can do great things by setting goals that go beyond partisan obstructionism and inspire innovation. Furthermore, it can do this in an effective and efficient manner.

> The average citizen's perceptions of government are perhaps most influenced by the employment practices of the federal civil service. We all probably have friends or relatives who are, or were employees of the federal government. The federal civil service evolved to address an environment of cronyism, where jobs were terminated or filled based on politics and not merit. This gave a bias to making federal civil service employment stable and merit driven. At the very top of the federal bureaucracy, where agency heads are appointed we still have a cronyism component, the most obvious recent example being ineffective handling by the Federal Emergency Management Agency , or FEMA, when hurricane Katrina hit New Orleans. By and large, however, federal civil service employment is stable and merit driven as intended.

For the past 30 plus years, middle class workers in the private sector have faced stagnant total compensation, and increased employment risk due to jobs being shipped overseas, or company downsizing, or outright bankruptcy. At the same time federal worker total compensation relative, to the private sector, has crept ahead. According to a 2010 analysis by the Congressional Budget Office, or CBO, the average total compensation package for federal civil service employees was higher than comparable employees in the private sector. For those with a high school education total compensation was 36 percent higher. For those with a bachelor's degree total compensation was 15 percent higher.

If we are to rebuild, and bolster the middle class, we have a good starting point in a federal employee class of citizens that are doing well. This fact however, must be accompanied by tangible government activism and policies to bring the private sector class of citizens that aren't doing so well up to risk and education adjusted total compensation levels comparable to that of federal employees. Without this, federal employees become by association de facto members of the political elite controlling our dysfunctional government to serve their self-interest rather than the common good. Without this, characterizing threats to federal total compensation as advocating a "race to the bottom" is unfair and more like "trickle down" economics talk - i.e. take care of federal employees and by some unspecified magic miracle it will trickle down to private sector employees. Successful governments and societies are built on shared expectations built over time by continuous effort to eliminate mismatched and less than fair myopic and elitist expectations.

Assessing how "efficient" government is, and where fraud, waste, mismanagement, and nonconformity to government policy exists is a major step toward the continuous improvement of government. Fortunately the US Federal government has been doing this for many years via the use of inspectors general, along with a supporting workforce totaling some 14000 employees. In 2008 Congress further bolstered these efforts with the creation of the Council of Inspectors General on Integrity and Efficiency, or CIGIE. The CIGIE consists of 73 inspectors general along with 6 members from the executive branch. In their 2012 annual report to the President and Congress, the CIGIE tallied 36 billion dollars in potential cost reductions, 10 billion dollars in potential additional revenue, 8,141 audit reports, 27,237 investigations, 623,623 hotline complaints, 6,669 indictments, 5,374 successful prosecutions, 1,069 civil actions, 5,805 suspensions or debarments, and 3,432 personnel actions. The CIGIE further outlined near term goals including the identification of major government vulnerabilities, opportunities, and best practices. All of this is a significant effort to manage government in an efficient manner. If there is a problem here, it is that all this effort mainly goes unnoticed by the average citizen because it doesn't get much media attention. This is perhaps because "small government" proponents don't want news on improvement efforts to be common knowledge, and/or "big government" proponents don't want news on major problems uncovered to get out.

Assessing and improving government "effectiveness" is more difficult than assessing and improving government "efficiency". Faced with a constant election cycle churn, agencies are forced to shift priorities and focus, leaving many laws and regulations looking like so much dead wood - i.e., unlikely to be enforced or energetically pursued, but nonetheless, requiring at least nominal resource and concern. On top of this, there are often multiple agencies that can be factors in a given situation. This of course leads to "a maze" of uncertainty by those in the private sector potentially affected by laws and regulations. This in turn becomes a drag on economic growth. To counteract this, Presidents have issued executive orders to agencies to seek public comment on modifying burdensome laws and regulations. As a general rule, however, law makers and regulators are not geared to "sun-setting" laws and regulations, and as we saw with financial deregulation and the repeal of Glass Steagall, their occasional efforts are corrupted by money'd special interests.

A more pernicious view of this situation is that dead wood or not, there are ample laws and regulations on the books for someone in government to go after and intimidate perceived enemies. This is of course a main contention for libertarian small government proponents. In 2013 for example, there was much controversy over the IRS handling of tax status for nonprofits associated with politics. So while there is some degree of truth in libertarian thinking, just having a smaller government does little to address the potential problem. Rather, we must rely on our Constitutional rights and an independent Judiciary to mediate legal and regulatory abuses. Beyond this, perhaps there should be an independent and permanent part of government that concentrates on clarifying and "sun setting" laws and regulations in a rational manner.

➢ From 1986 to 1995 about one third, or more than 1,000, of all US Savings and Loans failed. This has been termed the S&L crisis, and it cost taxpayers some 130 billion dollars in bailouts. Savings and Loans focus on making residential mortgages. The early 1980's saw lobbyist driven deregulation of the S&L industry which opened the door for risky activity beyond simply placing residential mortgages. A big bonus / get rich atmosphere came into play among S&L CEO's. Even then private libertarian economist and soon to be Federal Reserve Chairman Alan Greenspan got in on the deregulation with a study resolving that this risky activity was not harmful. But it did prove harmful in that S&L's borrowed their operating funds short term while lending it out long term. When short term rates rose dramatically, many S&L's became insolvent. Some S&L's covered up the insolvency with creative accounting that showed healthy profits and growth that ultimately defrauded investors attracted to the bogus healthy profits and growth.

Lincoln S&L was one of the large savings and loans that failed during the S&L crisis. When federal regulators started to investigate Lincoln S&L for fraudulent practices, no less than five US Senators put pressure on regulators to back off. The CEO of Lincoln was eventually sent to prison for five years while the US Senate Ethics Committee held hearings on the conduct of the five Senators. All of the Senators had received major reelection campaign money tied to Lincoln S&L. Senate ethics standards do not permit official actions "linked" with "fund raising" (wink). Hand slaps resulted as one Senator was reprimanded, two were criticized for acting improperly, and two were criticized for poor judgement. The S&L crisis did result in over 800 criminal convictions.

Contrast this with the more current 2008 / 2009 near apocalyptic financial meltdown where there have been a miniscule number of criminal convictions. Do we not have politically connected elites who are not subject to the law? Do we not have a government that does not enforce laws and regulations, because it does not want to appear anti-business since this would dry up political funding? **Has too big to fail been expanded to include too big to jail?**

> Privatization is the shifting of functions traditionally done by government to the private for profit sector. Privatization is done under the ideology that government is inefficient and the private market driven sector can do better for less cost. On the plus side there are examples of success, such as Elon Musk's rocket company SpaceX. On the minus side there is much that needs to be thought out. As a case in point, consider privatization of prisons which has become a booming business since the 1980's when mandatory sentencing and the "war on drugs" led to prison overcrowding. The US now has more than 2 million adults incarcerated in federal and state prisons. With only 5% of the world's population, the US has more than 20% of the world's inmates, with blacks and Hispanics being the bulk of that number. The US has the highest incarceration rate in the world, far outdistancing 2nd place Russia and our neighbor Canada which had a rate less than 1/6 of ours. We as a society have to take a serious look at our prison and drug policy because we have a problem. Privatization did not create this problem, but it will deter us from taking this serious look at changing what we do because that may be bad for business. In the coopted revolving door, over lobbied world we now live in power and political elites, and not society in general, will decide what that society looks like and it will be highly skewed by a slippery slope of profit motive. We have separation of church and state to protect freedom -

should we not also have separation of corporations and state for the same reason?

➢ In 1954 the percentage of men age 25 to 54 in the work force, i.e. those who either have a job or were looking for a job, was 97.9 percent. By 2016 the percentage had dropped to 88.6 percent. Researchers speculate the nation's high incarceration rate may give many men a problem with red flags raised during employer background checks, i.e. some 20 million Americans, mostly men, have felony records.

➢ In 2000 Portugal, with 1% of the population being addicted to heroin, had one of the worst drug problems in Europe. The government of Portugal studied the problem and decided to decriminalize drugs. Furthermore, they redirected funds formerly used to cut addicts off and disconnect them from society, and applied those funds to initiatives that would reconnect addicts with society. Included in these initiatives were programs for job creation for addicts as well as micro loans for addicts to set up small businesses. These programs have reduced drug use in Portugal dramatically, with injection drug use cut in half. Almost no one in Portugal wants to go back to the old system. A significant point here is the importance of good jobs and small business opportunities in building a healthy society that doesn't marginalize large portions of the populace.

The intelligence gathering budget of the US National Security Agency, or NSA, was beefed up significantly in response to 911 to prevent terrorist attacks. A large part of what the NSA does comes from private contractors. Booz Allen is a major NSA contractor and source of the "Snowden" expose on extensive computerized "big data", communications monitoring. Since "Snowden" we have found NSA guilty of overreaching, including major affronts to 35 world leaders that were being spied on. Given we have opaque computer systems with access to "big data", and more than 1 million government and private contractor employees with security clearances, it is likely that the NSA will be problematic and detract from the liberty loving society we want to be. In 2012 the National Defense Authorization Act, or NDAA, was passed by Congress. This act authorizes the military to put any US citizen into indefinite military detention if they are suspected of having any involvement in terrorism **- i.e. no lawyer, no jury, and no judicial system.**

The prior six chapters discussed major problems we as a nation face. In the next five chapters groundwork is laid for a simple change to our governmental system that can have far reaching effects in solving those problems. These next five chapters expand Common Sense 2.0, leading to Directed eDemocracy.

"It is not that I'm so smart. But I stay with the questions much longer." - Albert Einstein

"Ignorance more frequently begets confidence than does knowledge: it is those who know little, not those who know much, who so positively assert that this or that problem will never be solved by science." - Charles Darwin

"That is just the way with some people. They get down on a thing when they don't know nothing about it." - Mark Twain

CHAPTER 7

COMPLEX ADAPTIVE SYSTEMS SCIENCE

Scientists are now just beginning to understand and formalize "Complex Adaptive Systems Science". **As the term implies, "Complex Adaptive Systems" adapt, else they would not continue to successfully exist.** At the core of this new multidisciplinary science is the concept that our universe and life in general, exhibits recurring properties; a network of interactions "self organizes", adapts, and leads to a progression of ever higher levels of organization. Examples of this include, biologic ecosystems, ant colonies, the human body, the human brain, economic systems, social systems, the global internet, and last but not least governmental systems.

> ➢ The Santa Fe Institute is a multidisciplinary research center for complex adaptive systems science. The Institute was founded in 1984 by researchers from nearby Los Alamos National Lab. The Institute serves as an intellectual worldwide hub, fostering links to a wide ranging mix of

researchers in fields such as physics, mathematics, biology, and social sciences.

> Perhaps the best example of a complex adaptive system is our human bodies. Only 1 in 10 of our cells are genetically our own. There are thousands of types of microorganisms that coexist within our bodies in an ecosystem of shared expectations. By definition an ecosystem is a network of interconnecting and interacting parts. In return for interconnecting and interacting with these microorganisms, we share the expectation that they will help us with important bodily functions such as digestion and cell energy. At an intermediate level are of course the networked clusters of cells that are our bodily organs. At yet a higher level is our brain, which networks some 100 billion neurons. Humans in turn belong to societal networks, which with the dawn of the internet are "self- organizing" to become the networked "global" brain.

What follows could take an entire book to develop, but it captures the essence of complex adaptive systems. Many readers are not used to reading science textbooks, which can be compared to reading the assembly instructions for a piece of "you build / assemble" furniture. In the following scientific discussions many new terms and concepts are built and assembled. This of course requires time and dwelling / thinking on every term and concept. I have tried to write more at a science narrative level, which requires less time and less dwelling.

> Physicists use the concept of "entropy", which basically states that unless work is done on a system it will go to an unorganized, totally random state - i.e., pop a balloon with a pin and you will see the concept of entropy in action. The balloon is a boundary separating concentrated air from the

ambient random air. The balloon boundary enables work to be done concentrating the air. Take the boundary away and randomness takes over. So what brings us here as humans some 14 billion years after the biggest balloon pop (big bang) of all time? Complex adaptive systems science provides the answer.

As mentioned previously, a major concept of complex adaptive systems is that they "self-organize". I develop four terms / concepts here which are "self", "self-organize", "input-process-output", and "shared ecosystem". First of all, to "self-organize" you need a "self". A "self" comes about when a boundary develops that separates the "self" from its environment. The first primordial life form "self" arose out of a chemical soup environment as a hydrocarbon based soap bubble. The soap bubble served as a boundary, and inside the soap bubble was the first primordial "self", busily concentrating chemicals across its boundary. Once you have a "self", you can look at the organize part of "self-organize". You need something to organize with - i.e., another "self". A second, slightly different, primordial soap bubble happens, and the first "self" can now "self-organize" with this second, slightly different "self". How do these two "selfs" organize with each other? They must interact with each other somehow. In a primordial chemical soup environment, interaction comes in the form of "sharing" chemicals with each other. Each "self" soap bubble concentrates certain chemicals by allowing them to pass from the chemical soup environment across its soap bubble boundary i.e. "input". Inside the "self" concentrated chemicals are more likely to bounce into each other and "process" new chemicals in abundance. These abundant new chemicals are "output" across the soap bubble boundary to the chemical soup environment where they can be "shared" with other, slightly different soap bubbles. So we have the first soap bubble outputting in abundance chemicals that the second soap bubble likes as input, so it can in turn process and output in abundance chemicals that the first soap bubble likes as input. A network of "input-process-output" interactions has just "self-organized" in a "shared ecosystem" consisting of the primordial chemical soup, the first self, and the second self.

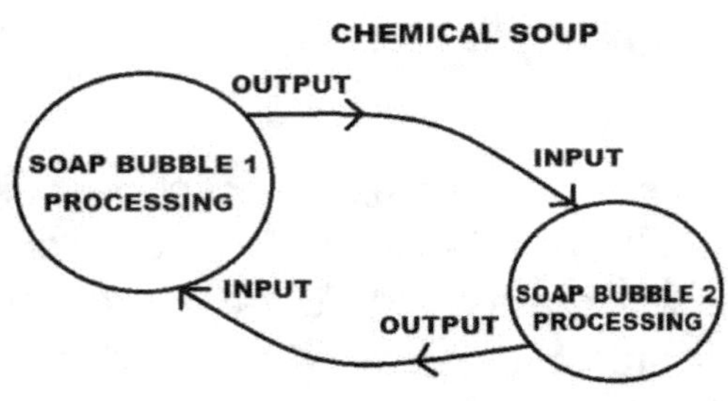

THE PRIMORDIAL BEGINNING

I develop three other terms /concepts here which are "sensing", "cognition", and "progression where the whole is greater than the sum of its parts". Our two soap bubbles "sense" each other's presence when there are certain abundant chemicals present at their soap bubble boundaries. Suppose the first soap bubble normally sits in the chemical soup all by itself, occasionally inputting across its soap bubble boundary the chemicals it likes to concentrate and process. Now suppose that the second soap bubble appears on the scene, outputting the chemicals it likes to output - all of a sudden the first soap bubble "senses" the second soap bubble is out there because the chemicals it likes as inputs are available in abundance . The first soap bubble now has abundant inputs and processes abundant outputs that the second soap bubble likes. In like manner the second soap bubble now "senses" that the first soap bubble is out there. When both soap bubbles sense each other we have "self-organized" a network of interactions and this creates "cognition". By definition "cognition" is the mental process of knowing, including aspects such as awareness, perception, reasoning, and judgement. We have "cognition" because the two networked soap bubbles know the other soap bubble is out there. Higher level cognition depends on lower level sensing. **It follows that**

the quality of cognition depends on the quality of lower level sensing. Also note we now have a "progression where "the whole is greater than the sum of its parts", since we now have two soap bubbles producing lots of chemicals that they would not be producing otherwise. So "self- organizing" has taken place via "sensing" leading to "cognition", leading to a progression to greater shared chemical "input-process output" levels across the "shared ecosystem".

I develop six other terms/concepts here which are "probability map of the environment", "signaling", "feedback", "foresight" , "adaptation", and "shared expectations". Suppose something in the chemical soup makes soap bubble two periodically shut down for a while. Furthermore suppose there is a third type of soap bubble in the chemical soup which is identical to soap bubble two in all but one respect, i.e. it produces the same outputs as soap bubble two - periodically shuts down like soap bubble two - but doesn't respond at all to soap bubble one's outputs. Soap bubble one only likes to boost output if soap bubble two is out there to respond in kind by boosting outputs that soap bubble one likes as inputs. Soap bubble one does not like to boost output if only soap bubble three is out there, because there is nothing to be gained by doing so. This creates an uncertainty for soap bubble one, and requires it develop a "probability map of the environment" to process an optimal output scenario. Soap bubble one's "probability map of the environment" is as follows - If I have a lot of inputs that I like then either soap bubble two or soap bubble three are out there. If I "signal" by boosting my outputs, and I don't see a big increase in "feedback" inputs then it is probably soap bubble three out there and I will reduce my outputs because there is nothing to gain. If I "signal" by boosting my outputs and I do see a big increase in "feedback" inputs then it is probably soap bubble two out there and I will keep my outputs at high levels because there is a lot to gain. With the "probability map of the environment", "signaling", and "feedback", we have a progression in cognition beyond just knowing to perception, reasoning, and judgment. Soap bubble one's "probability map of the environment" represents a progression in cognition that allows it to perceive, reason, and judge the probabilistic future with "foresight", and thereby supports successful "adaptation" to soap bubble three's presence. In our ecosystem consisting of chemical soup and three types of soap bubbles we have three different "probability maps of the environment" that reflect three different expectations. **The ecosystem not only shares chemicals, but also "shares expectations". To the degree the ecosystem has "shared expectations" coming from accurate "probability maps of the environment", the entire ecosystem can adapt and progress to higher levels of cognition, foresight, and optimal outputs. On the other hand, mismatches in "shared expectations" retard adaptation and progress to higher levels of cognition, foresight, and optimal outputs.** Over eons of adaptive time the boundary soap bubble becomes a cell membrane, becomes a multi-cell organism, becomes an organ in a multi-organ "brained" organism, ..., becomes a societal human in an increasingly interconnected and networked complex adaptive system.

> ➤ The functioning of brain neural networks depends on a chemical system called the dopamine system. Dopamine is a drug-like neurotransmitter that reinforces positive over negative experience thereby supporting the development of probability maps.

> ➤ The importance of networks of interactions can perhaps best be understood with the button/string analogy. First of all imagine taking a hand full of buttons and dropping them on the floor. Buttons represent the "selfs" in the ecosystem. Next cut a string into varying lengths short to long. The cut strings will be used to randomly connect 2 buttons together, and represent interactions between button "selfs". Notice that as you go about randomly connecting buttons 2 at a time with strings of varying length not much happens at first in terms of strings crossing each other - if you lift one of the buttons you will probably not pick up too many other buttons.

At some point however you "hit the elbow in the curve" and the number of buttons you pick up with a button dramatically increases - a button network complex adaptive system where the whole is greater than the sum of the parts has just "self-organized". Also note that in this mix of short and long strings, long strings are very important in helping the process along. Long strings can be thought of as long distance direct connections between buttons as opposed to connecting via intervening buttons. Long connections give our button network the "small world" property. You may have heard the supposition that to contact any person in today's world via friends to friends networks, you would only need to use six intervening friends networks. This makes for a "small world" and it comes via long distance connections which enhance both connectivity and speed.

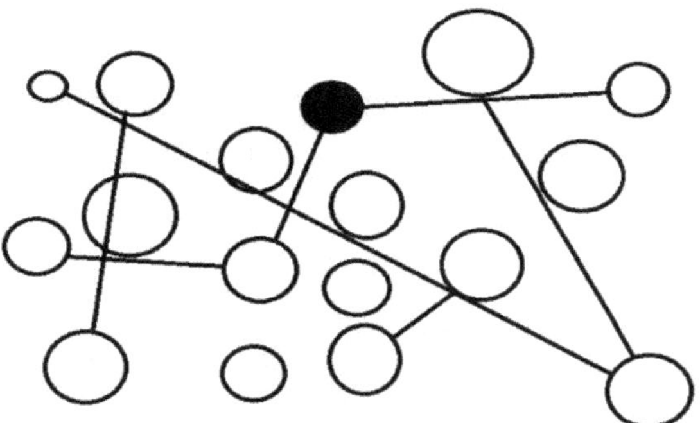

BUTTON / STRING ANALOGY

> Perhaps the best example of probability maps driving adaptation is baseball's Oakland A's. With a player payroll $1/5^{th}$ that of big money teams the A's consistently win by applying probability statistics to player personnel decisions. This was made famous by the movie Moneyball, starring Brad Pitt, depicting how in 2002 A's general manager Billy Beane cobbled together under valued misfits and cast offs to win the American League West, and set a modern day win streak record of 20 games.

I develop four other terms /concepts here which are "diversity", "exploration", "exploitation", and "flow". Recall that our soap bubbles exist in a chemical soup. The term chemical soup is used because it implies a "diversity" of many different chemicals. Chemical "diversity" enhances the opportunity to "explore" a myriad of chemical interactions, and thereby enhances the probability that complex adaptive systems will self-organize in the chemical soup, which is becoming a shared ecosystem of soap bubble selfs. **At some point some elite soap bubbles dominate the shared ecosystem by "exploiting" certain abundant chemical inputs to create certain abundant chemical outputs. This of course diminishes the relative diversity of the chemical soup, and thereby diminishes "exploration" which diminishes self-organizing and the progression of the entire shared ecosystem. "Flow" is the correct balance between "exploration" and "exploitation". Much like the carburation on an auto, "flow" can be neither too rich nor too lean, else the auto will not run properly.** So progression of the entire shared ecosystem occurs with a balance between exploration and exploitation, which is also a balance between cognitive growth and optimum outputs.

I develop three other terms / concepts here which are "phase transition", "decentralized", and "centralized". All this discussion of chemical soup and soap bubbles implies one thing, and that is that **"life" primarily involves at a conceptual level liquids as opposed to gases and solids. Liquids provide a concentrated yet freely mobile middle mode of networked interaction not available with solids which are less freely mobile and gases which are less concentrated. At all levels of complex adaptive systems there is a very important "phase transition", not unlike the phase transition from "gas to liquid" or "solid to liquid". In this "liquid" concentrated yet freely mobile middle is where networked progression takes place. Vary too far toward the gaseous or "decentralized" and networked progression ends. Vary too far toward the solid or "centralized" and networked progression ends** as well. The sweet spot for networked progression is in the middle between "decentralized" and "centralized".

> When human children are born it is without a "self". The "self" develops with experience, both good and bad, gained in the environmental ecosystem the child lives in. The child develops a "probability map of the environment", boiled down from the assessed probability of good or bad occurring in any given experience. To the extent this map accurately reflects the shared expectations of the child's environmental ecosystem, the child shows "cognitive growth" and prospers via abundant outputs to the environmental ecosystem.

Environmental ecosystems can be complicated, large, and ever changing, so "cognitive growth" has an important component called "exploration". Children, of course, demonstrate what seems to be an inordinate amount of "exploration", which is ultimately a search for subsequent adult focus. The biologist's view of exploration means a search of the environment to find promising niches to exploit. If exploration activity is too low, a "self" is likely to miss more promising niches, and get stuck exploiting a less promising niche. If the environment changes, this "self" will not likely be able to adapt by exploring for another niche to exploit. If exploration activity is too high, a "self" may find a promising niche but never exploit it. **So cognitive growth and optimum outputs occur with a balance between exploration and exploitation.**

I develop the term / concept of "eternity network brane" here. The term membrane generally means a layer, or sheet, forming a boundary. Physicists working on string theory coined the term "brane" to describe what is, in essence, a boundary layer, or sheet, as well. It is a dimensional layer, or sheet, where bounded measurement and observation takes place, the primary example being space as we know it which is a three dimensional xyz "3-brane". Branes can be thought of as open exploratory yet stable platforms for further networked progression in the universe over time. Obviously life as we measure and observe it progresses over time in xyz space, which is a "3-brane" that has existed for some 14 billion years. Einstein's space-time is therefore an "eternity network brane". Are there other "eternity network branes" as well?

Soap bubbles that have spent their entire lives focused on progression don't like to die. The eons of history behind progressing complex adaptive systems tells us that dying is probably not how it was meant to be, at least in the sense that progress is conserved. So there must be an "eternity network brane" related to life as we know it at work. What is this "eternity network brane" made of? The only answer for soap bubbles coming from a chemical soup is that this "eternity network brane" is made up of chemicals. Where is this "eternity network brane" located? Since "eternity network branes" relate to the soap bubble "self" not dying, they are located in the soap bubble. So we have an "eternity network brane" consisting of chemicals that exist in the soap bubble. There must be something special about these chemicals. Eternity implies these chemicals are long lived, and at their core don't change. So these chemicals are special in that they don't change in the face of all the other chemical interactions going on within the soap bubble. It just so happens that there is a class of chemicals called catalysts that have all these special properties. In fact this is the basis for DNA, which is certainly an "eternity brane" spanning multiple lifetimes, and moreover we are finding that DNA operates more like an evolving network than a simple set of on/off switches. So DNA is a true "eternity network brane". Emergent DNA in the soap bubble represents the part of a probability map that supports progression and is at or near 100 percent certain, and therefore it is a good thing to save for eternity. In fact some .1 percent of human DNA never reaches 100 percent because it is "remixed" in offspring in a form of continued exploration of probabilities. This ups considerably the ability to explore the environment, with diverse combinations of DNA, for niches to thrive in. So with DNA we have an open platform for progression, or "eternity network brane".

> As you may recall from the button/string analogy, network connections that are "direct and long" can have a more dramatic effect than adjacent connections that are "indirect and short". Direct long distance network connections relate to exploring an environment far and wide. They expedite finding more promising niches to exploit, and avoid getting stuck exploiting a localized less promising niche. Biologically speaking, unisex species waiting strictly for a single important random mutation to occur in their DNA went extinct because they were high on exploitation and low on exploration and could not adapt and evolve. Species having male and female however, with offspring getting half their DNA from each parent, "shuffle the DNA deck" with every offspring - in effect upping exploration of the environment using a myriad of possible DNA combinations. In humans this means lots of genetic diversity in offspring coming from the .1% of our DNA that is unique to every individual. This concept is not unlike the primordial chemical soup, i.e. it is a genetic soup.

> Both breadth and depth of exploration are important. Breadth of exploration relates to the novel remixing of what already exists. Mixing of DNA in offspring is an example of this. Businesses that repackage existing technology in novel useful products are another example. Depth of exploration relates to creating something totally new. Genetic mutations, and in modern times genetic engineering, are examples of this. Government and business basic research is another example.

The progression of complex adaptive systems depends on exploration balanced with exploitation. We have seen from the "soap bubble" discussion that certain "elitist" soap bubbles can take over and dominate the chemical soup with the chemicals they like to produce. This of course reduces chemical diversity in the soup to the detriment of exploration.

I develop the term / concept of "Cognition Net" (COGNET) here. DNA is not the only "eternity network brane" at work. As the progression of complex adaptive systems continued over the eons brains came about. Most of the cells in our body are not long lived. In fact over our lifetimes our body cells, and parts, are replaced in their entirety many times. The brain is an exception since it is where our probability maps of the environment exist. Brain cells are not prone to die since they are highly networked, and cell death would be bad for neural networks if we are to hold probability maps of the environment for future use. Our brains are therefore, part of an emergent "eternity network brane", not unlike the "catalyst chemicals" leading to DNA. Language followed by books followed by the networked internet, have made our brains part of an emergent "eternity network brane" that transmits to the future cognition that accurately maps the environment. I will call this emergent "eternity network brane" "Cognition Net" (COGNET). COGNET is of course an acronym for "Cognition Net" - but is also inclusive of the concept of a cog, in this case a big cog which powers the progression of the modern world. So we have three "eternity network branes". Space-time is the open platform brane supporting the subsequent DNA and COGNET branes. DNA works at a physical level and COGNET works at a mental, knowledge, and idea level. With modern societal man, the progression of complex adaptive systems has also led to government as a "self" in the COGNET. **Government legislation embodies a society's map of the environment. To the degree this legislation is an accurate cognition of the environment, government will survive into the**

future and be part of the emergent "eternity network brane" that is COGNET.

> Language is a very important open platform component of COGNET and can be considered a complex adaptive system in its own right. Language of course deals with storing and transmitting information. To be a platform language must be stable and hence comes with basic processes called grammatical rules. Grammatical rules provide syntax for stability that supports reliable communication. However languages are also living and creatively exploring, and therefore must be open and not overly prescribed by rules. In this sense communication of information is both constrained and probabilistic.

> As humans mature, gain experience, and build their "maps of the environment" their forebrain grows the most of any part of the brain. The forebrain is used in planning, decision making, moderating social behavior, and orchestrating thoughts and actions in accordance with goals, i.e., "executive functions". The benefits of these "executive functions" come at a cost. Humans use 20-25% of their basal metabolism on the brain as compared to 2-8% for most invertebrates. There are two types of limits on cognitive processing power. One type of limit is cost, which can a metabolic cost for humans, or a budgetary cost for societal man inclusive of governments. A second type of limit is natural physical as in the speed of electrical impulses and the heat generated by computer chips. Limits to processing power at any given network node have controlling effects on the structure of complex adaptive systems. The first effect is the use of probability maps of the environment to speed processing of an optimal output decision in any given situation. Neuroscientist's have determined that background maintenance of these probability maps consumes as much

as 20 times the energy as the actual conscious life of the brain. If a given situation is in our probability map of the environment, we can get a quick optimal output decision with little processing. For novel situations not mapped to our environment we require more processing, so we may "sleep on it". In fact it is during our almost mandatory daily sleep cycle that our brains do much of the maintenance to our maps. The second effect of limits on processing power is the distribution of processing power to lower level "sensing" network nodes, which feed higher level "cognition" network nodes via long distance connections on an exception basis when certain threshold signaling levels are exceeded. This makes the entire **"distributed"** network **"small world"** as discussed previously in the button analogy. This also makes the **"distributed"** network **"scalable"** to large sizes via use of multiple hierarchical levels and intermediate hubs.

> The following discussion relates to and expands on the prior discussion. Our "map of the environment" determines how we interact with the environment - i.e., our personality. Psychologists use the Myers-Briggs Type indicator to categorize a given personality. Myers-Briggs uses as paired dimensions introvert / extrovert (I / E), sensing / intuitive (S / I), thinking / feeling (T / F), and perceiving / judging (P / J) to define 16 personality types. These personality dimensions are tendencies, since in any given unique situation an individual could act out of tendency. Introvert personalities tend to synthesize cognition based on the knowledge and concepts coming from their personal internal networks of brain neurons. Extrovert personalities tend to synthesize cognition based on the knowledge and concepts coming from their personal external networks of people. Sensing personalities concentrate on concrete sensory data input. Intuitive personalities concentrate on abstract data pattern input. Thinking personalities concentrate on processing facts and principles. Feeling personalities concentrate on processing personal and interpersonal considerations.

Perceiving personalities concentrate on output that fits a "pliable" "map of the environment". Judging personalities concentrate on output that fits a "non-pliable" "map of the environment". Notice that the major complex adaptive system components are there - network, input, processing, and output. The personality dimensions that are most prevalent are extrovert 72% and sensing 74%. The other dimensions split 50% / 50%. The different personality types are found to predominate, and do well in different "career ecosystems"

▷ Some 1/3 of all House Representatives and 2/3 of all Senators are lawyers by trade, making "lawyering" the largest Congressional occupational block. This makes sense of course since legislation is law. According to Myers-Briggs, lawyers tend to be ENTP personality types. Among the strengths of this personality type are creative expediency and dealing with the politics of institutions. Among the weaknesses are impersonal detachment and low focus on implementation details. At the extreme these weaknesses feed a borderline unethical "find the loophole, game the system, win irrespective of right or wrong" mentality. It also feeds legislation tossed over the wall to implementers with little commitment to effectiveness and efficiency.

From a "lawyering perspective, the theatric media frenzy partisan "courtroom" that Congress is lacks one major component - and that is a citizen jury of "voter deciders". Well, we do have that - but that jury only meets every two years to vote and kind of sort of decide who won the myriad of intervening partisan debates / battles. Between those two years we have another jury made up of career politicians who are tampered with by lobbyists, and in effect, bribed by big money. Certainly lawyer legislators can understand we need to have more citizen "voter decider" jury presence to have a just political and governmental system - **i.e., in "courtroom"**

The following is a summary list of properties of "Complex
Adaptive Systems"

- Selfs that network, input, process, output
- Self - organization
- Progression to higher levels of organization
- Coevolution with ecosystem of shared expectations, leading to a whole greater than the sum of parts
- Exploration with flow across diverse and direct connections
- Processing power and cost constraints
- Higher level cognition with quality of cognition dependent on network structure
- Maps of the environment defining personality

"A primary object should be the education of our youth in the
science of government. In a republic, what species of knowledge
can be equally important? And what duty more pressing than
communicating it to those who are to be the future guardians of
the liberties of the country?" - George Washington

CHAPTER 8
SCIENTIFIC ANALYSIS OF GOVERNMENTS

How does government relate to the properties of "Complex Adaptive Systems"? First of all **government is a "Complex Adaptive System"** that networks branches of government, government bureaucracies, special interests, citizen groups, lower level governments, and foreign entities. Government entities take inputs through this network, process it, and create outputs. While the structure of the main branches of government is fairly well fixed by the DNA of government, Constitutions, the structure of all the rest self organizes around probabilities of good and bad under the impetus of legislation. The progression to higher levels of government is evident; witness the United Nations, European Union, World Trade Organization, and G20. **Governments, to varying degrees, coevolve with their networked ecosystem, or go extinct**; witness most Communist governments except China, whose government policies have led to dramatic economic growth over the past 30 years, a space program, and emergence as a world power. Governments have exhibited exploration, with flow across diverse direct connections beyond government; witness the development and widespread private sector use of the government incubated internet and global positioning system. Governments face processing power constraints in the form of cost as a percent of the total economy; witness ongoing government budgetary battles. Governments to varying degrees show quality higher level cognition with network structures connected to a depth and breadth of lower level sensing; witness China, which despite lacking democratic processes, still has direct polling connections into the populace with feedback acted upon at higher levels for the common good. Governments develop maps of the environment defining personality, witness the US whose maps are flawed and have led to a dysfunctional, maladaptive governmental personality.

> An eclectic global analysis would be remiss if it did not take a look at the consistent phenomenal success and economic growth of China. At the base of China's success is a Confucian ethic where government is seen as a necessary virtue (as opposed to necessary evil) to be run by the meritorious and enlightened. **Over the past 30 years China's annual economic growth rate has been about 3 times that of the US, translating into a corresponding improvement in the living standards of its people. China is on track to rival the US as a world power.**

On the negative side China is not without problems – the primary ones being corruption, political persecution, pollution, superfluous infrastructure projects driven disproportionately by debt, and a reputation for less than fair trade practices. Much of China's early rapid economic growth could be attributed to industrializing a relatively undeveloped economy. Being run by one party, the Chinese Communist

Party (CCP), and not being a democracy with popular voting, seems to contradict all present day recipes for success. On the plus side, the CCP has fully embraced their own form of capitalism. The key to China's success is the CCP's network structure and input-process-output mechanisms. First of all the CCP is a meritocracy with three career paths, and progression through four hierarchical levels. The career paths are social organizations, state owned enterprises, and civil service. The hierarchy starts with 900,000 CCP careerists at the lowest level and winnows down to 300 at the highest level CCP central committee. As I will discuss later, the network structure is a hybrid model skewed toward centralized. Centralized structures are prone to errors of commission as evidenced by Mao's cultural revolution when millions died. Hybrid network structures are capable of significant input-process-output and information processing leading to sound policies based on significant cognition. In the CCP's case this information processing comes in the form of extensive and frequent polling, accompanied by statistical analysis. Going even beyond this, the CCP has started a "monitory webocracy", where local officials get instantaneous feedback via "weibo", the Chinese version of "twitter". CCP member/official reviews and promotion is based on successful use of this information. Polling, "monitory webocracy", and meritocratic practices functionally replace their democratic counterparts of voting and winning elections. One could argue that polling and "webocracy" in an authoritarian and propagandized media controlled atmosphere will squelch diverse constructive feedback, and this is certainly true in areas that might challenge the unitary legitimacy of the CCP. But on the whole, the CCP's polling, webocracy, and meritocracy is geared toward making the lives of the populace better, thereby enhancing legitimacy. **The Chinese governing process is not unlike the extensive use of advisory referendums, and internet feedback, acted upon by a Board of Directors from a long term goal driven, strategic point of view.**

> The current conflicts over global warming and climate change give us an insight as to how China's governmental processes work. In 2006 China passed the US as the major source of CO2/greenhouse gas emissions. Moreover in 2006 China's CO2/greenhouse gas emissions were increasing dramatically while those attributable to the US were declining. In 2007 a Chinese opinion poll showed that 88% of the populace was concerned about climate change and 93% thought the government should do something about global warming. **In 2007 the Chinese government was the first developed country to develop and publish a national strategy for global warming.** Since some 40% of global CO2 emissions come from coal power plants and half of that or 20% is from China, coal power plants became an area of focus. **Fast forward to today and we find that China is the world's largest producer of wind turbines and solar panels.** China now has more than 150 Gigawatts of renewable energy capacity and has a goal of providing 16% of its energy from renewable sources by 2020. Because their requirements are so large and ever growing, China is still building coal power plants, but it has significantly shifted to renewables. The wind and sun are however uncontrollable. To get to more pervasive use of renewables China, and the rest of the world, has to solve energy transmission and storage problems in an inexpensive and large scale manner. Interestingly, the energy storage solution could involve a synergistic pairing of sea water desalinization along with hydrogen electrolysis where we'd get fresh water along with energy storage capability.

There are two properties of "Complex Adaptive Systems" that are at the core of political conflicts over government. First of all, governments have "a personality" based on their "maps of the environment and ecosystem" embodied in legislation. In the US two political parties have two disparate "maps of the environment and ecosystem" that are in conflict with each other as they vie to become legislation. Thus we have a split personality that will be dysfunctional and maladaptive to the degree shared expectations cannot be negotiated. Secondly, government, as essentially the "brain of society", has cost constraints similar to the way the human brain has metabolic cost constraints - i.e., a highly cognitive brain is desirable, but has to justify metabolic cost with enhanced success in adapting to the environment. In this context the US federal government has major problems since it exhibits suboptimal cognition, high costs / deficits, and an inability to adapt.

In the US the Republicans favor a decentralized small government whereas the Democrats favor a centralized big government. From a global perspective in terms of government spending as a percent of an economy, the US sits in the middle, with countries such as Cuba at the "big" end, to countries such as Afghanistan at the "small" end. The "sweet spot" appears to be in the middle. Taking a "Complex Adaptive Sytems" perspective, which viewpoint is right - Republican or Democrat? First of all, neither of these is right, because these views are over simplistic. The decentralized/centralized small/big attributes do however serve as a good starting point for a discussion. Add to that discussion starting point the fact **we want the entire societal ecosystem of shared expectations to progress to higher levels of success. To use the button /string analogy; we need all buttons to be connected and pulling up. The whole becomes greater than the sum of its parts. The right discussion flows from this mind set.**

> "Personality" relates to a free will and choice. Ants don't seem to have a personality. Cats seem to have an "introverted", somewhat independent personality - don't even try to herd them. Dogs seem to have an "extroverted", somewhat dependent personality - try walking a dog, and keep them from checking out the "calling cards" of other

dogs. In fact, in higher level "Complex Adaptive Systems" such as humans, more "personality", free will, and choice are exhibited. Humans, via free will and choice, exhibit an unprecedented range of behavioral responses to their networked ecosystems, ranging from classical music to monster trucks. This of course comes from goals beyond species survival, and focuses on following goals, aptitudes and interests. Moreover humans are capable of modifying the focus of the actual networked ecosystem they input-process-output with. While this focus can have benefits in pursuing high goals, it can also lead to problems - the proverbial "blind spot" and dysfunctional maladaptive personality. The "blind spot" can occur because the pathway to that part of the networked ecosystem is weak, or because humans, having free will, choose to minimize input from that part of the networked ecosystem; perhaps because of some prior bad experience that happened, and possibly coupled with some addictive focus of escape. This leads to narrowed, incomplete, and inaccurate "maps of the environmental ecosystem", and therefore an inability to input, process, and output successfully in other than the part of the network in focus. **"Blind spots" created by focus can be compensated for by a more direct connection to those parts of the networked environmental ecosystem that are "out of focus".**

➤ Brains themselves vary, often in a less than optimum fashion. ADHD (Attention Deficit Hyperactivity Disorder) is evidenced by inattention, hyperactivity, impulsivity, and lack of focus. Certainly the US government exhibits this disorder by jumping between two parties every election cycle, then going into gridlock after an initial honeymoon period. At the other extreme is autism, which is evidenced by an over focus, often at the expense of connectedness to what is going on generally. Certainly the US government, where the average "in session" congressional work week has shrunken to 2 days because focus is on raising reelection money from money'd lobbyists and wealthy elites, exhibits this property. In fact while in Washington a typical congress person spends almost half their work day just down the street from the capitol building at call centers set up for cold calling potential fat cat political campaign donors - something that is illegal on the actual capitol building grounds itself! **We want and need a cognitive government with fewer symptoms of ADHD and autism.**

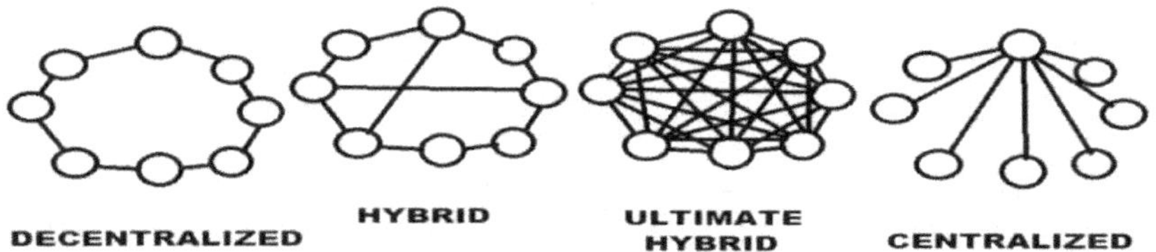

As illustrated, the three basic types of network structures are decentralized, hybrid to ultimate hybrid, and centralized. Strictly speaking, the hybrid to ultimate hybrid structures are three dimensional multilevel which makes them both **"small world"** and **"scalable"** as discussed in the previous chapter. The real world example for a decentralized system is an ant colony. Ant colony cognition is low because it is all "ant to ant" sensory without higher level processing and cognition. The ant colony does however do well in its own narrow map of its environmental ecosystem, as if "guided by an invisible hand" (think Adam Smith and free market capitalism). Having low cognition, and personality, means the ant colony is unlikely to progress to higher success levels because it is low on exploration to expand its narrow map, leading to missed opportunities, and "errors of omission" across the networked environmental ecosystem of shared expectations. The real world example for a centralized system is "pure" Communism. Communist cognition is low because it is mainly centralized, "hub" processing without lower level sensory processing (exception modern China). Low cognition and personality means that Communism is unlikely to progress to higher success levels because it is low on exploration to expand its narrow map. Being guided by a centralized "hub" means the survivability of Communism is subject to centralized "hub" malfunctions, and processing power constraints, which can lead to "errors of commission". Centralized "hub" dependence makes it unlikely Communism will survive long enough to progress over the long run to higher success levels. **Hybrid systems represent the "sweet spot" between decentralized and centralized where cognition, and personality, are optimized for success across the networked environmental ecosystem of shared expectations.**

From a governmental standpoint, network structures are hybrid. Libertarian decentralized regimes don't exist and elitist centralized regimes don't last. The question then arises, what tools can be used to look at a government to tune it to the sweet hybrid spot, and optimize for success. I develop here the inter-related concepts of "boundary conditions", "mind experiments", and "thought constructs". Scientists often use "boundary conditions" to narrow focus and gain insight into phenomenon. A boundary is a discontinuity. Some boundaries cannot be crossed, while others can be difficult to cross because conditions on the other side vary dramatically. The speed of light, for example, is one boundary whose conditions were explored in "mind experiments" by Einstein to open up much progress in science. Einstein's "mind experiments" of course, led to the cognition that since the speed of light cannot be exceeded (i.e. it is a boundary) there is convertibility between mass and energy. "Boundary conditions" are also used in the "natural" sciences. For example, we have seen how the "laffer" curve used 0% and 100% tax rate "boundary conditions" to justify the "thought construct" of supply side economics, and focus on lowering tax rates. This overly simplified, single factor analysis proved antithetical to actual experience which should have also looked at demand, and the "laffee" curve "thought construct" using wealth concentration boundaries of 1 family and 150 million families. Following from this, is the idea that our main tool for understanding government is comparative analysis using "thought constructs" that look at conditions in relation to the decentralized and centralized network structure boundary condition extremes. This offers "nuanced views" of where in the hybrid range a government operates. The following is a list of those "thought constructs".

NETWORK STRUCTURE THOUGHT CONSTRUCTS

Decentralized (Boundary)	Hybrid	Centralized (Boundary)
⬇	⬇	⬇
Low Cognition	Max Cognition	Low Cognition
Data	Data & Goals	Goals / Ideology
Omission Errors	Lower Errors	Commission Errors
Conflict	Peace & Shared Expectations	Conflict
Self serve	Servant Leadership	Hub serve
Libertarian	Man - Spirit - God	Elitist

The first thought construct is cognition. Nations with the best cognitive government have the best "fitness metrics" across a broad spectrum, inclusive of societal as well as economic "fitness metrics" / well-being. We have seen how the US lags many nations in important areas and the trends are downward. Among the fitness stars is Switzerland. Interestingly, if you asked a Swiss what it is about their country that they are most proud of they would say their democratic system, which has been evolving for more than 800 years. **The Swiss democracy fits the cognitive model well, and most notably is a two way street "direct democracy" using voter referendums and initiatives.** Nations with the best cognitive government also show foresight that takes action. Unfortunately the US governmental system has two opposing "maps of the environment", and is incapable of further "brain processing" to reconcile maps such that action follows. **The Swiss do not have a single executive-president, but rather a** seven member executive-federal council - not unlike a Board of Directors with a lead director. By convention the federal council is inclusive of four political parties - i.e., four "maps of the environment". The federal council has proved capable of further "brain processing" to reconcile maps such that action follows. Beyond this, action items can be taken directly to the Swiss people via referendum. So the US has suboptimal cognition, and needs more "brain processing" capability to reconcile maps such that action can be taken.

> Sir Francis Galton was a half-cousin of Charles Darwin, and a polymath, meaning he was a person whose interests and expertise had a wide spectrum. One summer Galton was at a country fair where several hundred people were in a contest to guess the weight of a butchered ox. To Galton's astonishment the median guess of the crowd was within 1 percent of the actual weight. Since Galton's time there has been much theoretical work on the "wisdom of the crowd". **Essentially there are certain favorable conditions under which the "wisdom of the crowd" emerges. First there has to be diversity of opinion. Secondly there must be a non-elitist equality of opportunity to independently espouse opinions over an adequate non-rushed time span. Thirdly there must be a systematic mechanism to turn collective judgements into a collective decision.** These are precisely the conditions embodied in Directed eDemocracy, a concept of government to be developed in subsequent chapters of this book that enhances adaptability. Unfortunately Galton supported social Darwinism, which is elitist and contradictory to an ecosystem of shared expectations

> The term "well connected" is often used in discussions of the elite of a society. It implies advantage unavailable to the non-elite in developing and applying their talents. **Networked connectedness is an important and desirable aspect of**

complex adaptive systems to the degree it does not have an adverse impact on the diversity necessary for continued exploration and progression of a society. Maintaining diversity means fostering networked connectedness beyond just the elite. Doing so allows the non-elite to develop and apply their talents such that the entire societal ecosystem prospers.

The second thought construct is whether emphasis is on data, data & goals, or goals / ideology. At the data extreme is thinking that free markets controlled by price data mechanisms are the solution to everything. This marginalizes higher order societal goals such as, from a historical perspective, eliminating slavery, or from a modern perspective, providing health care to all. At the goals / ideology extreme, we have the opposite thought condition where goals are pursued and data, especially data contradicting the ideology, is marginalized. We get socialist ideologues pushing a welfare state and ignoring fiscal data, or "Ayn Rand" ideologues pushing hands off capitalism and ignoring data showing pervasive crony capitalism and an elitist marginalization of entire classes of citizens. All of the above are evident in US government. Moreover the country is whipsawed and gridlocked into ineffective and inefficient government, always battling the most immediate crisis. **We need to move to the hybrid middle where we can reconcile two opposing maps of the environment and come up with long term shared goals with progress managed continuously using the most relevant data available.** Our societal "self" development thrives only when the proper network, input data, and goal driven processes are in place to generate optimum outputs for all in the ecosystem of shared expectations.

> Ayn Rand was an American philosopher and novelist. She was born and raised in Russia where her father's business was confiscated during the communist revolution. She

emigrated from Russia to the US where she advocated limited government and "hands off" capitalism. This is perhaps an example of the flip side of government promoting the common good, in that in the process of supposedly promoting the common good, government induced trauma was inflicted on entire classes of citizens. In Ayn Rand's case it resulted in her narrowed map of the environment where all government is bad. Ironically this narrowed map of the world made it to the present day where it has led to supply side economics and government induced trauma to the poor and middle class. Strictly speaking this was more of a creeping trauma since it took some 30 years. Conflict arising from government induced trauma, is to be avoided, since this does not serve this purpose of shared expectation development. **Truth and trust result from the ongoing process of small steps to develop shared expectations taken in a transparent manner with persistence over time.**

➢ In more recent times Social Security has added a welfare component which includes Social Security Disability Insurance or SSDI. SSDI recipients are also eligible for Medicare. The SSDI screening process was liberalized in 1984 such that there has been a dramatic increase in the number of people receiving SSDI payments. Projections are that some 7% of the nonelderly population will be on SSDI. Moreover, SSDI disability, which should be somewhat homogeneous across the country, shows regional concentrations. Much of the growth in SSDI has been for mental illness and bad back disability, which can have a degree of subjectivity. Are people gaming the system? Probably. The bigger issues is a society in which a large segment of the population is only marginally engaged, and in fact financially jeopardizing the Social Security and Medicare programs which meet real needs for a large segment of the population.

The third thought construct is omission/commission errors. On the commission side, the second Iraq "preemptive" war with projected costs of more than 1 trillion dollars, thousands of wounded and killed, no weapons of mass destruction, and terrorist spawning insurgent instability in the middle-east, shows too much centralization, at least in the area of executive war making functions. More "checks and balances" seem to be warranted. On the omission side, the near financial collapse of 2008-2009, which occurred against a backdrop of financial deregulation pushed by money'd special interest lobbying, shows too much "hands off" decentralization in our government, at least in the area of legislative regulation of entities crucial to our societal and economic fitness. Interestingly in parallel with this "hands off" governmental policy is a too big to fail, "centralized" financial industry which our model tells us is prone to errors of commission, such as what happened in the near financial collapse of 2008-2009. In this regard "more government" that is not coopted by money'd lobbying is warranted to mitigate nongovernment, centralized concentrations of power prone to errors of commission. **So in "nets-speak", we need a "self" in our governmental network that enhances our system of checks and balances and diminishes the insidious influence of money.**

The fourth thought construct is conflict versus peace. Conflict exists at the decentralized (example - Afghanistan) and centralized (example-North Korea) extremes. Those extremes have suboptimal network connections and weak input / processing / output functionality. **Peace exists in the "adaptive" middle where a networked ecosystem of shared expectations exists. Conflict is of course a major mismatch in shared expectations. To reduce conflict, mismatches in shared expectations have to be addressed. This can take time since it requires building network connections along with inputs, processing, and outputs. This leads to improved cognition via better "maps of the environment".** Reducing mismatches in shared expectations also means eliminating closed secret processes in favor of open transparent processes. Our US partisan gridlocked small versus big governmental conflicts certainly point to a need to move toward the hybrid middle and shared expectations. We need to enhance network connections to citizen voters along with improved input / process / output mechanisms. **To develop shared expectations closed secret money'd lobbyist driven processes must be replaced by open transparent processes driven by citizen voters.** Over the long run the Internet is a boon to all of this conflict reduction since it is all about networking people, knowledge, and concepts. Over time governmental cognition will improve and provide a base for global success via better maps of the world environment. Proponents of conflict in the form of protest, such as the Occupy and Tea Party movements, highlight mismatches in shared expectations, **but to the detriment of their causes, offer solutions in the context of the current political and governmental system which institutionalizes political inequality, and thereby compromises the long term sustainability of any victories they might have. To diminish the need for protest we need substantive structural changes moving us towards the "hybrid middle" which fosters shared expectations, political equality, and less conflict.**

> ➢ Climate change and greenhouse gas emissions get a great deal of attention relative to the potential for "nuclear winter" resulting from nuclear conflict. Yet nuclear holocaust driven by conflict and/or error can occur in an instant with major ramifications. Perhaps more effort should be put into diminishing the nuclear threat to human existence.

The fifth thought construct is whether emphasis is on the decentralized self, or centralized hub. From an economic perspective this relates to an "Ayn Rand" keep government from getting in the way emphasis on the self and individual initiative, versus big government controlling "human excess" that detracts from the "common good". The middle perspective is that everything exists in a societal ecosystem, and empowerment of individual initiative is fine as long as mismatches in shared expectations are negotiated away, often with the help of government leadership as it serves the societal ecosystem and common good. From a governmental perspective we see both self and hub emphasis in the US. People are elected and reelected to Congress to represent a district or state. No one is elected to Congress to represent the entire nation. We have seen how this translates into pork and national debt which puts Congress at the self-serve end of our construct, at least when it comes to pork associated with reelection. But wait, we have a two hub, or two party system, where one party is "in power". In Congress this comes in the form of party leaders who enforce and "whip" fellow party members of Congress to "serve the hub". **Remember a hub system's operations are susceptible to loss of a hub - well our system of government is always going to have one lost hub. Moreover this lost hub is often trying to sabotage operations of the other hub on purpose.** So we have grid lock by design, but perhaps too much gridlock? The political elite like this arrangement because it offers bountiful "deal making" opportunities from which to prosper. **The solution is a third hub that does not go offline, does not sabotage, and is representative of the long term interests of the entire nation. The constraint is that it must be a "tweak" that the more tractable political elite will support.**

> ➢ The "sweet spot" between self-serve and hub serve is servant leadership. Servant leadership is both a philosophy and set of practices. In fact there are universities with degree programs focusing on servant leadership. Servant leadership is rooted in a need to serve rather than an ego driven need for money and power. Servant leadership philosophy encompasses shared power, putting the needs of others first and helping people develop and perform as highly as possible. The most important part of leadership is making good decisions. Leading groups in the wrong direction can

be highly destructive.   Thus "effective" leadership trumps "efficient" leadership.   Servant leadership, as a system, provides a non-elitist networked ecosystem orientation that is conducive to making good decisions.

The sixth thought construct is man - spirit - god. This is a rather large and comprehensive topic since it involves religion, so the next chapter is devoted to it.

"I know no safe depository of the ultimate powers of the society but the people themselves; and if we think them not enlightened enough to exercise their control with a wholesome discretion, the remedy is not to take it from them, but to inform their discretion by education. This is the true corrective of abuses of constitutional power." - Thomas Jefferson

"My concern is not whether God is on our side; my greatest concern is to be on God's side, for God is always right." - Abraham Lincoln

"I know not with what weapons World War III will be fought, but World War IV will be fought with sticks and stones." - Albert Einstein

"Reading furnishes the mind only with materials of knowledge; it is thinking that makes what we read ours." - John Locke, Philosopher

CHAPTER 9

MAN – SPIRIT – GOD

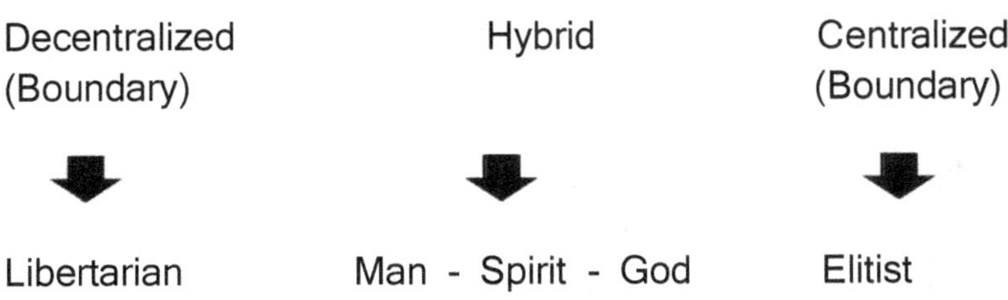

As mentioned previously, this chapter is closely related to the prior chapter which used thought constructs to analyze how well our government was functioning as a "Complex Adaptive System". The sixth thought construct, which is Man - Spirit - God, proved to be an expansive discussion, so this separate chapter was split out. For your convenience I have repeated the prior chapter's Decentralized-Hybrid-Centralized schematic above. Above left we have "libertarian" man who values freedom above all else since freedom is essential to achieving one of life's primary goals, which is to self-actualize.

> Abraham Maslow was an American psychologist who studied the motivations of "high achieving" individuals and developed the concept of a hierarchy of needs with basic physiological needs such as food, shelter, clothing at the bottom of the hierarchy and self-actualization at the top. **Individuals who are not having basic physiological needs met (i.e., poverty) are not going to move up the hierarchy of needs to self-actualize. High achieving societies are societies where as many motivated individuals as possible are pursuing high achievement and self-actualization.** In the early 1800's political thinker and historian Alexis de Tocqueville toured America and wrote "When both the privileges and the disqualifications of class have been abolished and men have shattered the bonds which once held them immobile, the idea of progress comes naturally to man's mind; the desire to rise swells in every heart at once, and all men want to quit their former social position. Ambition becomes a universal feeling." **If you believe America is the land of opportunity and every American is entitled to the opportunity to pursue success then that entitlement is based on a lower level entitlement to have basic physiological needs met. In this context we as a society must eliminate poverty. Entitlements to end poverty should not be viewed as a sign of societal sickness, but rather as a sign of societal health since we are fostering motivated individuals who can pursue self-actualization. Freedom is required to pursue success and self-actualization to the utmost, and this includes freedom from an intergenerational cycle of poverty.**

Freedom is unconstrained if man is by himself. Add a second man to start forming a society, and freedom is constrained since that second man comes with a second set of expectations of what the societal relationship and progression should be. So as the number of individuals (both men and women) in a society increases individual freedom will decrease as expectations are shared amongst the many. Freedom loving libertarian man tolerates this to the degree there is a benefit coming from the societal system. If expectations are not shared and/or parts of society do not benefit from the societal system, conflict arises. Low level conflict that irritates individuals is normal and healthy as part of the continual societal process of adjusting societal expectations. Governments arise to manage and reduce this conflict, and this is really a process of adjusting and setting shared expectations. Governments develop laws to codify established societal expectations. However, laws are skewed towards the expectations of those making the laws, and this has typically been "elitist" entities with disparate military and/or economic power. Historically the net result of "elitist" lawmaking has been that what is legal and what is moral are not always the same. **In this context morality means the minimizing the freedoms constrained proportionate with the maximizing of societal benefits received by the entire diverse societal ecosystem.** A prime example of the disconnect between law and morality is the Supreme Court's pre Civil War 7-2 Dred Scot decision when Chief Justice Taney stated blacks "were so inferior that they had no rights which the white man was bound to respect". So basically slavery was legal under the Constitution - but it certainly wasn't moral because it negated the freedoms of whole classes of people - thus the schematic at the beginning of this chapter showing libertarian and elitist interests at the extremes of societal progression. Libertarian decentralized network structures are mostly lower level sensory input with little higher level cognition. Elitist centralized network structures are mostly higher level cognition with little lower level sensory input. **Societal progression comes from maximum cognition of what is going on in the society and this comes between the libertarian and elitist extremes via the hybrid network model.** Less than optimal network structures lead to less than moral laws created in an environment of elitist political inequality. This in turn creates major conflict to the degree expectations of individual and societal benefits are not met and there is less freedom. This is where Man - Spirit - God and religion comes into the picture.

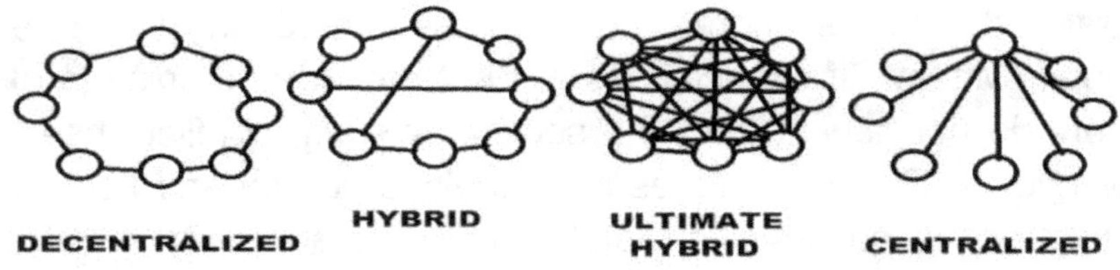

NETWORK STRUCTURES

Religion can be viewed as a check and balance to counter laws that are less than moral. The "religious spirit" can foster societal progression, and in fact offers god as the ultimate hybrid model to which both man and society are progressing. God as the ultimate hybrid model has complete and perfect sensing and higher level cognition of the societal ecosystem and therefore maximizes societal benefit while minimizing constraint of individual freedom. This in turn leads to minimum conflict since shared expectations are being developed and met. **Thus societal progression is a move towards the ultimate hybrid god model with extensive and direct network connections leading to maximum lower level sensing and higher level cognition.** This in turn leads to better systems of laws that reflect shared expectations. The term expectations implies probabilistic factors, which as discussed in prior chapters, means better systems of law that provide a better societal probability map to support better decisions via maximum foresight.

Historically government has shown a propensity to become controlled by the elite thereby stifling societal progression. Likewise, to the degree religion becomes intertwined with government, religion has shown a tendency to become elitist and stifle societal progression. At the extreme we have a theocracy where there is ecclesiastical control of government such as in some Islamic states. These states tend to have suboptimal network structures skewed towards centralized elitist. Their network structures are suboptimal both internal to the state and the rest of the world. Complex adaptive system science tells us that this leads to lower cognition levels and more conflict. These states will tend to be left behind as the rest of the world progresses well beyond them. At another extreme we have an atheistic society such as formerly Communist Russia where religion has little influence over government. Communist China is not exactly in the same class as Russia since it has an underlying Confucian ethic that has some of the characteristics of a religion. To the degree atheistic states are not protected by constitutions and don't have an underlying religious like group ethic, they will also tend to have suboptimal network structures skewed towards centralized elitist. Complex adaptive systems science tells us that this leads to lower cognition levels and more conflict. Again, these states will tend to be left behind as the rest of the world progresses well beyond them.

➢ As mentioned previously, the Swiss have been evolving their direct democratic processes for 800 some years. The Swiss are at or near the top of world lists in various economic and societal metrics. **The primary focus of the Swiss however, is not on any particular political ideology for achieving any of these economic and societal metrics. Rather the Swiss focus is on their direct democratic processes which build political consensus, while at the same time deferring to and accommodating minority interests. The Swiss are most proud of their democratic system, and only by association the successful economic and social benefits derived from it.** The Swiss juggle a diverse mix of three major languages, two major religions, and resident population that is some 20 percent foreign. Over the years there has been conflict in juggling that diverse mix, but for the most part by modern times the Swiss had figured it out. One could say that Swiss direct democracy is closely associated with a Swiss ethic of public service, not unlike a Confucian ethic is closely associated with Chinese public service. The Swiss have ongoing "values training" in the form of universal military service for males (voluntary for females) over 18 years old.

From a complex adaptive systems perspective, the middle ground in all this is where government and religion are separated, but interact to develop "shared expectations". In the US, separation of church and state is provided for in the first amendment of the Constitution. The separation of church and state issue reached fever pitch during the 1960 presidential election when John F. Kennedy, a Catholic, was elected amidst election rhetoric that Kennedy would be a puppet of the pope. More recently the conservative religious right has been coopted with "values" rhetoric that has proved to be more talk than walk. Religion is separate from government, but since religion is part of the networked environmental ecosystem, it has a role in negotiating shared expectations. In this sense religion perhaps acts as a societal conscience and ethic, thereby serving as a check and balance against bad government, money'd special interests, and elitism.

> ➢ In late 2013, Pope Francis wrote his "Apostolic Exhortation", which essentially presented in great detail the Catholic "map, or view, of the world". Such "maps" are of course important because they are used to trigger matching future action. What Pope Francis wrote amounts to a "game changer", especially concerning the US. In fact Time magazine subsequently named Pope Francis "person of the year". Pope Francis is a Jesuit, and Jesuits are focused on the poor and marginalized members of society. The following four paragraphs "paraphrase" Pope Francis's views.

First of all Francis revitalized a progressive tradition in economics. Progressive economics holds that government spending on public works during economic recession is the best policy along with reduction in income inequality. Progressive economics dominated up until the stagflation 1970's when it was supplanted by "trickle down" supply side economics with an emphasis on growth. Trickle down efficacy has not been backed by the facts. Naïve trust in the goodness of those wielding economic power has led to a globalization of indifference. To the exhortation "thou shalt not kill" must be added the exhortation "thou shalt not have an economy of exclusion and inequality that also kills and excludes outcasts as leftovers. We cannot accept money's dominion over ourselves and society. We cannot accept a lack of concern for human beings where man is reduced to one need – that of consumption. We cannot accept government tainted by the corrupting influence of money.

Secondly, Francis stated that exclusion and inequality feed conflict, less security, and more violence. It is evil crystallized in unjust social structures, which cannot be the basis for a better future. Disintegration of the family and a drift toward individualism threaten important societal interrelationships. Beyond the family society must connect and integrate all "selfs". Political elitism must end.

Thirdly, Francis stated that Christianity requires that religion not be relegated to the inner sanctum of personal life without influence on societal and national life, without concern for the soundness of civil institutions, and without a right to offer an opinion on events affecting society. A major issue is inclusion of the poor and marginalized in society. We can no longer trust the unseen forces and the invisible hand of the market. We need responsible populism inclusive of dignified work, education, and health care. Responsible citizenship is a virtue, and participation in political life is a moral obligation.

Fourthly, Francis stated that certain principles will guide future strategies. "Time is greater than space" gives priority to initiating processes rather than processing spaces. In other words **new processes that support big picture long term goals should be emphasized over narrow short term immediate results that leave faulty processes in place.** "Unity prevails over conflict" stresses reconciliation of differences and creating new and promising synthesis. "Realities more important than ideas" means there will be a continuous dialogue between ideas and reality - i.e. truth. "The whole is greater than the parts" means our societal networked world model is like a polyhedron which reflects the convergence of all its peoples, each of which preserves its distinctiveness. **There must be a continuous dialogue between faith, reason, and science. There must be a reform of societal systems and ideologies, not just individual morality.**

Overall I would say there is quite a bit of resonance between the views of Pope Francis and "Complex Adaptive Systems Science". I found it particularly interesting that Pope Francis explicitly mentioned a connected polyhedron model, which is not unlike our ultimate hybrid or god model.

"Our government needs the church, because only those humble enough to admit they're sinners can bring democracy the tolerance it requires to survive" - Ronald Reagan

CHAPTER 10

DIRECTED eDEMOCRACY

Most people would agree that we need a democracy that can both take action to solve problems, and open up opportunities for a freedom loving citizenry to pursue. To do this we need a "governmental brain" with enhanced cognition, and extensive sensing across a broad networked ecosystem, most notably a citizenry that is diverse and politically equal. **To accomplish this I am proposing "Directed eDemocracy" as a simple low risk add on, or "tweak" to the existing system, that addresses many of our governmental malfunctions, and is entre to the Internet Age future. "Directed eDemocracy" comes from an eclectic selection of best democratic processes from around the world. "Directed eDemocracy" also has a solid scientific grounding coming from "Complex Adaptive Systems" science.** "Directed eDemocracy" is voter rather than money'd political elite centric, and pairs an elected independent board of directors working real time with voters using the internet as a governing tool. I start by discussing a conceptual diagram of the networked ecosystem that is our currently existing government. That conceptual diagram, which follows, is based on the previous discussions from prior chapters.

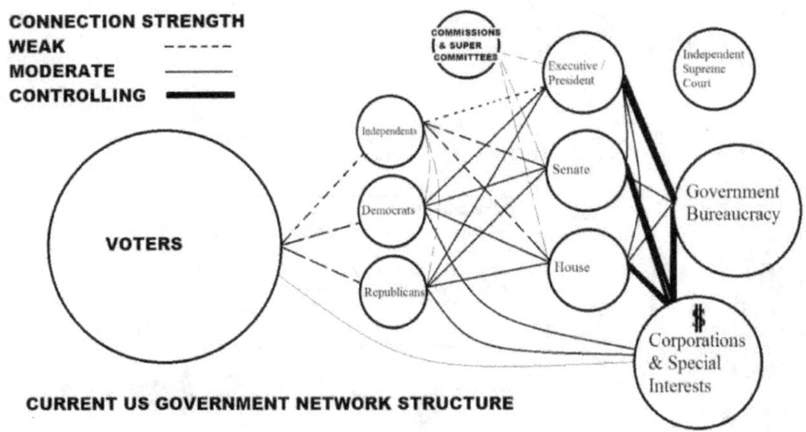

Notice where there are weak connections. Independent voters, which are about 1/3 of all voters, have weak connections to government. Another 1/3 of all voters, Democrat, or Republican, have weak connections to government depending on whether they were winners or losers in an election cycle. **So 2/3 of voters typically have weak connections to our governmental and political systems. It is not good for a representative democracy to have 2/3 of the voters with weak political representation.** Another area of weak connection is to the Supreme Court - but this is good because it has a focused "big picture" mission on Constitutional matters, and therefore needs independence from undue influences. This is under siege however, as an elite clique of Supreme Court Justice former associate's exhibits disproportionate success in having appeals heard for the business interests they tend to disproportionately represent over private individual interests. So in effect money'd special interests are lobbying the independent Supreme Court. In fact over the years the Supreme Court has shown a bias toward factional economic / political power as shown by the Dred Scott Decision in 1857 which basically said slavery was ok, and the more recent Citizens United Decision which basically said political inequality related to money is ok. The average voter connection into money'd special interests is weak because this area is dominated by big money and big corporations. **Money'd special interest connections into the House, Senate, and Executive (via the Government Bureaucracy) are strong and problematic when**

juxtaposed with weak voter connections. Also notice (top center of diagram) the weak connections of Commissions and Super Committees into the system. These tools of governance have been a more prominent feature in recent times as an ad hoc attempt to fix our malfunctioning governmental systems. I next discuss a conceptual diagram of the proposed changes to the governmental network.

> ➤ One of the big questions to ask is why more than 80% of congressmen win reelection while Congress itself often has an approval rating of less than 20%. One answer is voter apathy and alienation. Worldwide the US ranks in the bottom quartile for percent of voters voting. If you don't approve of Congress and you don't vote you probably feel the system is rigged and corrupted by money that protects the status quo and your vote won't matter. Furthermore, you probably don't have one issue that fires you up, and the litany of Democrat and Republican promises don't resonate with your thinking on all issues. Elections become a spending frenzy and a fight for the voters "in the middle".

Incumbents have two major advantages. First of all they and their staffs have spent much of their time in Congress making deals and raising money for reelection. Incumbents outspending their upstart opponents usually win elections. Secondly, to the extent they have garnered pork for their constituents, incumbents have ongoing good publicity that gives them name recognition - i.e., Congress may rate badly but "my representative" is good. The distinction in approval ratings is that Congress is bad for the country, but my representative is good for this small part of the country.

Term limits have been a much talked about idea to oust incumbents, and improve the approval rating of Congress. Given that this idea has been around quite a while and has gone nowhere, one suspects that elitist career politicians will never vote to end their own careers. DUH! Moreover most term limit proposals still allow more than one term, which negates many of the benefits of term limits. Career politicians do have a point that term limits would gut a lot of valuable expertise garnered from years of committee assignments. Lacking progress on term limits, voters have on their own accord taken a "vote em out" approach leading to the rise of the Tea Party. This movement seems to be topping out, and we are left with a small number of new faces with the same do nothing Congressional system. **We need to move to Directed eDemocracy and we need the help of the political elites to do this - the new George Washington will likely come from their ranks.**

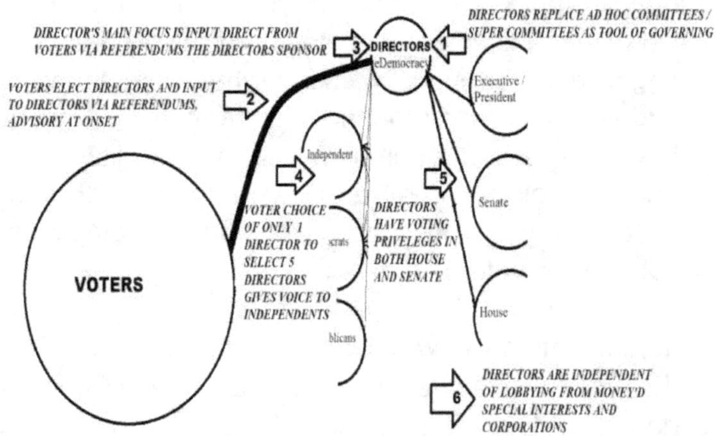

US GOVERNMENT FOCUS ON PROPOSED CHANGES TO NETWORK STRUCTURE

The following discussion relates to the prior numbered diagram which depicts proposed changes to the US government network structure to implement "Directed eDemocracy. This is more of an overview that will be expanded subsequently. First (1), with a Constitutional Amendment we have replaced the ad hoc Commission & Super Committee with an ongoing elected Board of Directors, with a focus on using eDemocracy as a tool of governing. Second (2), voters elect Directors and input direct to Directors via referendums which are advisory at the onset. Third (3), Directors main focus is taking input from voters via internet held referendums the Directors sponsor. Fourth (4), in a nationwide election voter choice of only 1 Director to elect 5 Directors gives voice to independents. In other words, an election ballot will list all Director candidates, and the voter can only vote for one. The top five Director vote getters are elected. Fifth (5), Directors cannot be ignored since they have voting privileges in both the House and Senate. Sixth (6), Directors, limited to a single term, are independent of lobbying interests, using primarily voter and public hearing input.

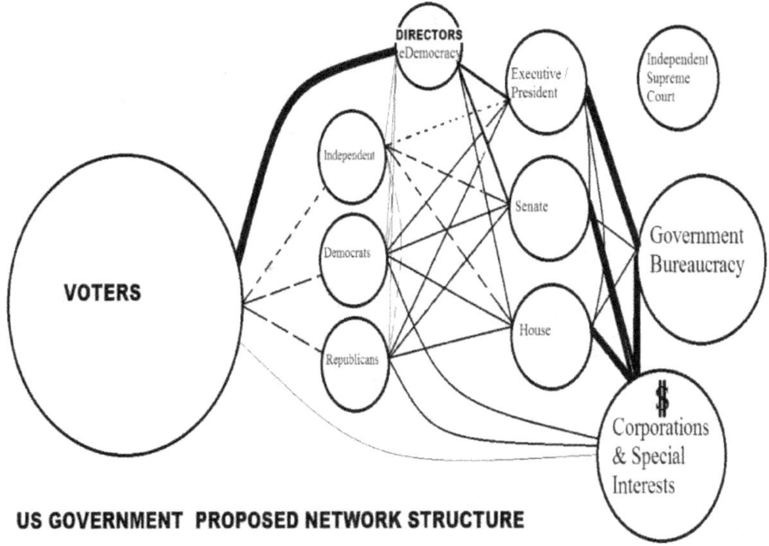

The preceding diagram merges the initial government network structures diagram with the proposed changes. The following discussion relates to the preceding diagram. Why have a Board of Directors? Modern organizations have a Board of Directors elected by stakeholders to help with big picture, longer term strategic matters. Should not our government have the same? Ad hoc commissions and super committees were weak attempts to cobble together a Board of Directors function. Lacking was the political clout coming from being elected, voter referendums, and voting privileges in House and Senate. By having directors elected nationally to single terms we have a governmental body more interested in solving national problems than garnering pork for home districts, or money from special interests for reelection.

At each election cycle, voters cast one director vote, with the top five vote getters being elected, so independents, representing 1/3 of the electorate, can now have a voice, and we can have honest debate, not filibustered or whipped into line. With independent directors, we have a resource to reconcile two opposing "maps of the environment" so action can follow. We also have an additional check and balance against legislation "pushed to the floor" with instructions to not debate, or amend. Since all these changes are a simple add-on to the existing system, we have a proposal that can garner support from the more tractable of the political elite - i.e., no term limits, or immediate threats to their reelection funding. In fact, the political elite get a new chance to serve, and perhaps a jump start to their political careers by serving as a director.

Why have eDemocracy along with a Board of Directors? We as modern, goal driven humans have a penchant for the latest tools. Should not our government do the same? **We are at the dawn of the Internet Age, and our modest eDemocracy proposals serve as a low risk entre into the future - it gets us started.** Advisory referendums taken via the internet give voters a newfound political voice that translates into Board of Director's clout with Congress, backed by director voting privileges in Congress itself. With eDemocracy we have an open ended governing tool that puts voters in control, and voting that actually counts for something, not just wishful thinking every two years. Advisory votes could even be taken on what referendums the public is interested in, in which case the process becomes more like what is called a "voter initiative" in political parlance. **By having eDemocracy paired with a Board of Directors we have mitigated a major "blind spot" towards voters in our governmental networked ecosystem, improved both the breadth and depth of our government's sensory input, added additional processing beyond simple "map of the environment" checking, and improved government cognition to foster improved outputs. As a big bonus, Directed eDemocracy diminishes the influence of big** money, since "buying a representative" means less if voters can ultimately have the final say on any given issue or policy – you can't buy off the entire populace.

> In the US elections are primarily the responsibility of the states, each of which has its own election commission / board. At the federal level we have the Election Assistance Commission (EAC) which was created in 2002 as an independent agency whose mission is to improve the elections process. The EAC developed Voluntary Voting System Guidelines (VVSG) and has federal funds to improve the administration of US elections. The EAC has conducted a survey of 32 internet voting projects in 13 countries. These projects range from pilot projects to fairly comprehensive operational systems. **The overall idea seems to be getting on the learning curve in a low risk manner, and thence expanding use of this important emerging tool for democracy as experience and comfort levels increase.** In the US, the first internet voting at the federal level will likely be a national primary for Directors of the new federal Board of Directors, with actual election using the traditional method of voting. Thence internet voting will be used on a regular basis for "advisory" referendums and initiatives, with ultimate legislation going through the traditional Congressional process with the exception there are now ten more "Director" votes in both the House and Senate, and these "Directors" have a primary focus on running, and using the national referendum and initiative system.

> Daily US political news coverage usually includes mention of some poll taken by any of a myriad of polling entities. These are "scientific" polls from the standpoint that the citizen sample is representative of the entire population, and thereby one can statistically give a validity range that is typically plus or minus a given percent. As we saw with gun control efforts

following the Newtown Connecticut tragedy, overwhelming polling numbers don't usually translate into Congressional action because the dynamics and culture are dominated by big money lobbying. Directed eDemocracy gives public sentiment a chance.

➢ All advisory referendums are not equal. Referendums that both present, and gather meaningful information at the same time are the best. By having a Board of Directors debate a referendum before putting it out to vote, we can present with the referendum a brief pro and con that voters can use to help them decide. This is especially possible with the internet since we can have a check box that indicates the pro and con section was read before proceeding to voting. We can also present variant alternatives to a referendum to discover some of the more nuanced preferences voters have. In fact, the process is not unlike polling, except that the sample is the entire nation, and it is more directly tied to the legislative process.
Some referendums can be "forced" by the populace independent of any legislator involvement. The Swiss "initiative" forces a referendum, but with a delay of 2-3 years to buffer short term political moods. The Swiss legislature gets to recommend for or against the "initiative", and also gets to offer an alternative to the initiative. The voter gets 2 votes – one for or against vote, and a second vote for the alternative the voter likes. Most Swiss initiatives have failed, however at the same time some sort of legislative response to citizen concerns has resulted.

The following lists and discusses point by point the details of Directed eDemocracy.

1. **Five Directors will be elected in a national election every two years with voters voting for only one director, and the top five vote getters winning election. National election**

means the Directors represent the nation, not a particular district or state for which to garner "pork". By having the top five winning election we expand voter representation beyond the party in power.

2. Directors will be limited to one four year term, thus with five directors elected every two years, there will be a total of ten Directors serving at a given time. By limiting Directors to one term we mitigate the influence of money for reelection campaigns.

3. Director elections will be held in odd numbered years. By holding elections in odd years we give focus to the national debate, and what voters expect of Directors. We create the possibility of getting things done in Congress without having to wait another year.

4. Directors will have voting privileges in both Houses of Congress. Thus there will be 10 more votes in the Senate and 10 more votes in the House. By giving voting privileges to Directors, we extend the prior but less than effective concept of ad hoc commissions and super committees, to more of an ongoing true Board of Directors function, with political clout coming both from being elected and having voting privileges in both the Senate and House. A powerful additional option might be to give the Directors the ability to force votes in Congress to counter gridlock attributable to committee chairman keeping things "bottled up in committee".

5. The main focus of the Board of Directors will be our budding Directed eDemocracy. Implementation starts with the internet being used to hold a national primary for Directors. A government-run campaign web site will be set up that provides tools for prospective candidates to briefly list their qualifications and policies, along with links to their own web site. National primary voting will be conducted using internet voting with the top ten vote getters going to a national election using the same traditional voting system we have always used. Periodically, from thence forward the Board of Directors

will conduct advisory referendums and initiatives using internet eDemocracy facilities.

6. The intent of the Board is to attract problem solving senior statesman. Certain Board candidates will automatically be eligible for listing on the government run campaign web site. These include former US Presidents, former US Vice Presidents, former members of Congress, and former State Governors. All others will be listed by opening up the internet voting primary early, and with a write in capability, such that names reaching a certain threshold can get listed on the government run web site.

> "Tyranny of the majority" is usually espoused by libertarian advocates as a major problem with democracy, and any plans to enhance it with more direct democracy. Japanese American internment camps driven by public furor during WWII is often used as an example, but more often than not libertarians are really centered on big government taking money out of their pockets, and eventually running up big debts at the behest of voters. To their discredit, libertarians can't point to one existing government that fits their small government model. Tyrannies are eventually stopped by our system of checks and balances and Constitutional Bill of Rights. In fact Directed eDemocracy raises the opportunity for minority interests, including libertarian, to be heard - another check and balance if you will. Since Directors represent national interests rather than a geographical area, and are limited to one term, they are less attached to excessive government spending tilted towards winning reelection. Furthermore, although the long term goal is true direct democracy, by starting with "advisory" referendums and initiatives attended to by a Board of Directors, we have the opportunity to set a tone that the process supports strategic direction, rather than trivialities gamed by big money and voters voting themselves overly generous benefits. Finally, referendums on divisive issues could be set up such

that a super majority of perhaps 60 percent voter approval is required.

> Related to tyranny of the majority is populism. Populism in its own right is mostly good to the degree it comes from an ideal of promoting the greatest good for the greatest number and doesn't trample over whole segments of the populace in doing so. Populism, however, that comes with a degree of elitism that could do some trampling over "non-elites" is dangerous. The most notable example of this is an elitist nationalist populism that ignores the furtherance of shared expectations amongst peoples and nations. Nationalist populism typically develops a narcissistic leadership bent on furthering the elitist populism thru manipulation of public opinion. This usually means focusing on some outside threat or wrongdoing accompanied with control over the news people get and coordinated programs of propaganda. In the absence of an independent judiciary with oversight over national intelligence / security resources one ends up with fascist governmental regimes, which are also indicative of and in response to failed democratic processes that feed public furor, frustration, and discontent.

> It would be a major oversight if "direct democracy" in California was not discussed. California has become the "poster child" for how "direct democracy" can become dysfunctional. Basically California initiatives and referendums, called propositions, have to a degree been taken over by big money special interests. The result has been increased spending, not balanced with tax revenue which has led to big deficits. Moreover, longer term focus on priorities is nonexistent, with symptoms ranging from more money being spent on prisons than education, to a crumbling infrastructure.

To correct this, a "Think Long Committee" with prominent personages was formed in 2011 to push reforms to the "proposition" process. The first reform is to adopt the very successful Swiss practice of requiring proponents of "propositions" to negotiate, and reconcile with the legislature. Lacking reconciliation, multiple alternatives would appear on a ballot along with ample, yet not overly long, education on each alternative proposition's merits. The intent here is to inject more deliberation into the process, independent of special interests. A second reform is to require more transparency as to who is funding each side. The intent here is to give voters an idea of what big money special interests are involved. A third reform is to undertake major tax reform, and "pay as you go" , where new spending is balanced by tax revenues or delineated spending cuts, and vice versa, tax reductions or caps are balanced by delineated spending cuts. The intent here is preventing "tyranny of the majority" from spending more and/or taxing less, which of course leads to crippling deficits.

The "Think Long Committee" would like to be made a permanent fixture of California government. In fact they would like to eliminate, and replace the California Upper House, or Senate, which has ceased to be a meaningful, deliberative, strategic view body, and is duplicative of the representative functions of the Lower House. I will call this new body a Board of Directors because conceptually that is what it is. Part of the vision for this Board is to have it direct scientific polling, much as the Chinese do, to foster deliberation leading to propositions and reforms. Another part of the vision is to give this Board subpoena power, and have it work with the California state auditor to audit spending, ultimately leading to "sun-setting" of certain laws and regulations.

All of this activity in California is very promising and mirrors much of what Directed eDemocracy wishes to achieve. Directed eDemocracy is more tuned into political realities, and therefore more likely to be implemented in an environment controlled by political elites who like the status quo. In addition, the Directed eDemocracy Board members, who are elected to a limited single term, will typically be inclusive of independent viewpoints. The California Board the "Think Long Committee" envisions is not elected but appointed primarily by the governor. This leaves the Board process under unitary control of the governor, which is a negative.

"When it can be said by any country in the world, my poor are happy, neither ignorance nor distress is to be found among them, my jails are empty of prisoners, my streets of beggars, the aged are not in want, the taxes are not oppressive, the rational world is my friend because I am the friend of happiness. When these things can be said, then may that country boast its constitution and government. Independence is my happiness, the world is my country and my religion is to do good." - Thomas Paine, Rights of Man

"We must not confuse dissent with disloyalty. When the loyal opposition dies, I think the soul of America dies with it."
- Edward R. Murrow, Journalist

"I must confess that I do apprehend some danger. I fear that they may place too implicit a confidence in their public servants, and fail properly to scrutinize their conduct; that in this way they may be made the dupes of designing men, and become the instruments of their own undoing. Make them intelligent, and they will be vigilant; give them the means of detecting the wrong, and they will apply the remedy." - Daniel Webster

CHAPTER 11

SHADOW GOVERNMENT - BRAINS & PERSONALITY

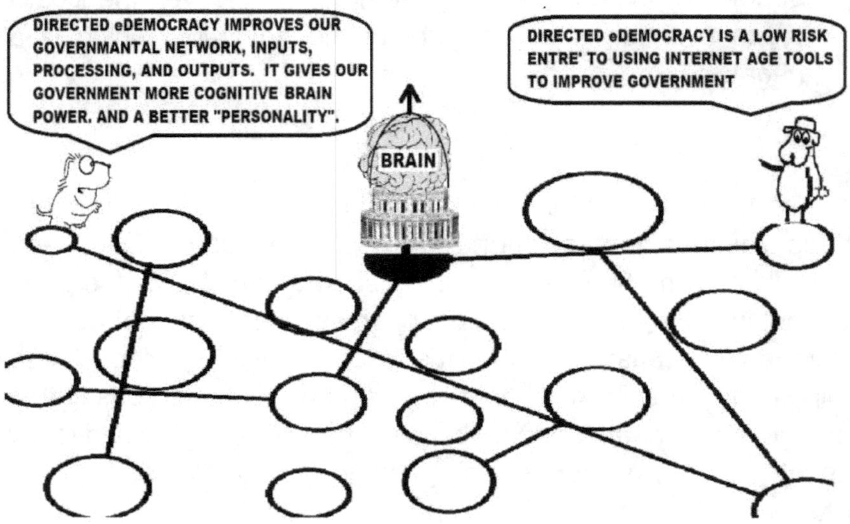

Given the innate inability of Washington to get anything done, what are the prospects for Common Sense 2.0 and Directed eDemocracy as developed in this book? I think they are very good. First of all, the political elites and the system they like are not being met head-on, and in fact the "new George Washington" will likely come from the more tractable of the political elite. Secondly, lacking action, it is likely a "shadow Directed eDemocracy" government will emerge that will show the way. A shadow government is a second government that operates in the shadows of observable government, and exerts or seeks to exert control over observable government. The term shadow government can have bad or good connotations. We already have a bad shadow government operating today in the form of big money special interests. To counteract this we may need a good shadow Directed eDemocracy government aligned with voter interests.

A shadow government is precisely what our American Revolutionaries set up in 1773 when patriot leaders from the thirteen colonies set up committees of correspondence to coordinate responses to Britain, and share plans. In the context of today, some enterprising patriot activist will set up this shadow government. In its simplest form this could be a web site that simply tracks, aggregates, and publicizes the results of the various national opinion polls (Gallup, JZ Analytics, Pew Research,...) and treats them like actual done deal referendums if they show overwhelming popular support within their scientific statistical margins of error. In a more expanded concept this web site could be exactly what the government would set up if it adopted Directed eDemocracy.   At the core of this web site would be internet voting – think parallels to the "like" function on facebook. The web site would have campaign facilities to elect a shadow government Board of Directors whose function would be to conduct advisory, internet voting "polls" (pseudo referendums and initiatives) on important issues. The "shadow" Directors could also vote in parallel with actual important votes taking place in Congress.   **In addition to internet voting, the eDemocracy would have two way e-consultation, e-petitioning, and e-discussion in a manner similar to what is being implemented in Switzerland.**

> A 2017 poll conducted by NPR/PBS (public radio/tv) found 60% of the public does not trust, to some degree, opinion polls. The same poll showed 37% of the public does not trust the media, and this perhaps underlies to a large degree the distrust in opinion polls. If we are to advance democracy there must be an advancement in shared expectations which means advancement in trust. Properly designed opinion polls should reveal the publics expectations, especially if they show overwhelming support on any particular issue. Outright referendums are however preferable to opinion polls, especially when the referendums are openly debated.

➢ Lacking a national referendum, numerous local communities put their own referendums on the 2016 presidential election ballot. For example in Wisconsin 18 local communities had an advisory referendum to amend the U.S. Constitution to roll back the power of unlimited money in our elections and clarify that only human beings should have inalienable rights, and money is not the same thing as free speech. The referendums were overwhelmingly passed with the average percentage win being 84% for the amendment. Why can't we do this on a national level?

➢ In 2011 the United Kingdom government set up a public e-petition web site. Citizens of the United Kingdom have a constitutional right to petition their government. In its first year of operation this e-petition web site averaged 52,000 visitors and 213,000 page views per day - all in a country of 60 million people. It took about 8 weeks and $130,000 to initially set up the site. The system has a citizen verification procedure that works very well. Any validated citizen can start a petition and any validated citizen can electronically sign any petition. When a petition reaches 100,000 signatures the issue can be selected for debate in Parliament. Links to social media sites make it possible for petitioners to promote their petition. Use of the governmental tool is still evolving, and the next step is setting up a committee of Parliament to take ownership of and direct the e-petition site and process. Scotland and Wales have set up similar sites. There are numerous other e-petition initiatives around the world including AVAAZ, an international activist network with more than 45 million users in 194 countries using 15 languages.

Once this shadow government web site gains popularity another enterprising patriot activist will emerge, and get involved in close congressional primaries and elections by throwing support to candidates supporting eDemocracy and following through in like manner with a voting history that is aligned with public opinion. In like fashion, the eDemocracy web site will likely set up a thumbs up / thumbs down page on congressional candidates depending on their support for eDemocracy. **Eventually, the "new George Washington" will emerge, and we will be on our way to a constitutional amendment for Directed eDemocracy.**

> ➢ Grover Norquist is a conservative activist who wields considerable clout with conservative Congressional legislators. Mr. Norquist founded and heads Americans for Tax Reform, a non-profit that coerces legislators to sign a pledge not to raise taxes else resources will be employed in opposition to their reelection. In 2012 some 95% of Republican legislators signed the pledge. The same tactics have been extended nationwide down to the state level. Although I am not enamored with this because it essentially promotes, in complex adaptive systems terms, a suboptimal decentralized "ant colony" governmental model, I am mindful that the same tactics can be used to successfully promote Directed eDemocracy which is a more optimal "hybrid" governmental model.

> ➢ The Constitution does not require that the Speaker of the House of Representatives be a sitting member of the House, thus a viable option for promoting eDemocracy would be for an eDemocracy movement to offer its own nominee for Speaker of the House of Representatives. Consequently if this nominee was not chosen an eDemocracy movement could give thumbs up / thumbs down to House members depending on their support.

At some point, some variants of what I propose for Directed eDemocracy will come up. That is fine as long as certain principles are inviolate. Those inviolate principles include, first of all having an independent Board of Directors elected to a single term by voters in a national election, and inclusive of independent and minority interests. Secondly, Directors will have voting privileges in both the House and Senate. Thirdly, that Board's focus will be using the internet as a governing tool, starting with frequent voter input via advisory referendums. Fourthly, via advisory referendums and public hearings, the Board will be a catalyst for meaningful public debate.

Direct Democracy purists may be asking why not just start with outright referendums and initiatives that are binding rather than advisory? I agree that this is the ultimate goal, but I thought it more important to get into the Internet Age because this is the future. The internet also gives us the ability to easily set up a "shadow government" with which to force the accountability of representatives to voter as opposed to big money special interests. This harnessing of voter backlash would also ultimately lead to a constitutional amendment for Directed eDemocracy.

Political Independents and more tractable Democrats and Republicans may be asking why not propose a political party that is "outside the box", and thereby beyond control of extremist ideologues and big money lobbying. Such a political party would be based more on Directed eDemocracy processes and developing long term shared expectation goals with effectiveness and efficiency "data managed" rather than "ideologue sabotaged". This party would not be small or big government, but rather ultimate hybrid network government. Some group of enterprising patriot activists will come forward to start this party. In fact it would become one of many "E2D" Internet Age Direct Democracy parties that have already been started internationally.

The current representative democracy was quite revolutionary when set up more than 200 years ago, but had little to do with actual popular vote since the President and Senators were "selected" by state legislatures. House Representatives were popularly elected, but only propertied white men could vote. **The point is we got on the learning curve and grew our democratic processes as our society progressed.** Internet Age Directed eDemocracy, starting with advisory referendums and initiatives, gets us on the learning curve without all the grousing over how secure or risky the internet is (despite the fact institutions such as banks routinely use it). **There are two reasons advisory referendums and initiatives can be just as effective as actual binding referendums and initiatives. First of all members of Congress with voting records that do not match up with advisory referendums and initiatives will be publicly accountable and subject to voter backlash. Secondly, provisions can be set such that controversy over advisory referendums and initiatives can be settled by actual binding referendums and initiatives conducted using traditional voting methods.**

Variants to the Directed eDemocracy proposed might include having the sitting President appoint one member to the Board while that President is in office. This might help in expediting reconciliation of differences with the executive that might preclude meaningful progress on an issue.

Another variant might include having both the House and Senate elect a sitting member to serve on the Board during a two year session. Again, this might help in expediting reconciliation of differences with the House or Senate that might preclude meaningful progress on an issue. As a positive side effect, if voting for this Board member is done by secret vote not subject to "the whip", we might foster an atmosphere of bipartisan problem solving in Congress, since election to the Board could be a career advancing political plum that would not likely be available to partisan hardliners.

A final variant might be having an actual national binding referendum vote triggered by approval in both the House and Senate. This might come from "naysayers" doubting the validity of an advisory referendum that looks like it will gain traction – but that is all well and good because it's a check and balance.

The first priority of the new Board of Directors would be to develop a core of shared expectation goals. This would be done via advisory referendum. A first shared expectation goal might be political equality. This would be inclusive of diminishing the influence of money in politics. A second shared expectation goal might be bolstering "The American Dream". This would be inclusive of increasing social mobility and reducing poverty. A third shared expectation goal might be governmental fiscal responsibility. This would be inclusive of ending accounting gimmickry, means testing entitlements, and ending "corporate welfare". A fourth shared expectation goal might be continuous improvement in government effectiveness and efficiency independent of whipsawed political interests.

> ➢ We have 50 states which theoretically, in our federalist system, can serve as experimental incubators for best government processes. Most recently the health care system in Massachusetts was used as a template for "Obamacare". Irrespective of how well Obamacare works out, a federalist approach to coping with what one views as nonperforming, unresponsive, and corrupted federal government is a viable option to pursue. At the extreme however, this can be seen as an attempt at "Balkanization", where big money is used to "game" the system and exploit political inequalities. The term

"Balkanization" means to divide into small quarrelsome ineffectual states that can be manipulated and controlled. Control state legislatures and you call the shots in gerrymandering federal Congressional districts - that gets you control of the House. To control the Senate concentrate on spending your political money where it goes farther - in small population, "small media" states. Top it all off with voter suppression "model legislation" and your political machine is hard to stop. This is all done under the "branded" guise that local "control" is best, even in matters that should be part of federal government "DNA". Faulty "DNA" leads to cancer. A balkanizing strategy, in fact, seems to be used successfully and controversially by the American Legislative Exchange Council, or ALEC, a nonprofit which despite claims to the contrary, represents Republican and corporate interests by pushing "model legislation" to state legislators, primarily via "educational junkets". ALEC has little interest in making our federal government better. Quite the contrary, an ineffective and inefficient federal government makes ALEC's call for limited small government stronger. Gut out the federal government, and ALEC's hand in shaping a federalist state based system becomes even more powerful.

The major problem with ALEC is that it does nothing for political equality because it is controlled by and pushes corporate special interests. They are guilty of major hypocrisies, including saying they are working at the state level because states are closer to the people – even though the average state citizen has no clue what is going on behind closed doors at those junkets. Though claiming to be for limited government, and by connotation less regulation and "free markets", they are actually a conduit for crony capitalism. ALEC's large, corporate, special interests push model legislation that favors their competitive interests over smaller upstart competitors. Small and limited government becomes a crony capitalist business opportunity to privatize. The question about what is best for our society becomes skewed by a cozy relationship with business interests pushing privatization. A look at states where ALEC has been most successful shows that they do tend to rank high for their business environment, but fair quite poorly when looking at societal metrics such as incarceration rates, poverty, and literacy. Despite their high rankings for business environment, this has not seemed to translate into "organic" job growth as evidenced by unemployment rates at best mid quartile. In fact "job growth" is mostly a zero sum game with governors seeking to take jobs away from other states.

So in net the main contentions with ALEC are that it is driven by money'd special interests, lacks transparency, and "games" political inequalities. What ALEC does contradicts progress towards the optimum "hybrid middle" where the US will continue to be a high functioning world leader, and in fact ALEC moves us more towards the decentralized ant colony model where corporate interests and power dominates the kind of society we want to be.

➤ In October of 2013 the federal government was shut down as Congress haggled over Obamacare and the debt ceiling. Polls showed the public had mixed views on Obamacare, but was overwhelmingly against government by crisis leading to shut-down and threats to the full faith and credit borrowing power of the federal government. The crisis was created in part by the Speaker of the House's refusal to bring a vote on the debt ceiling to the floor for a vote. In fact leading up to this point, the debt ceiling had been used for many years by the House as a bargaining chip to force any number of issues, not just Obamacare. In the following December of 2014 government shutdown was avoided, but only because a compromise bill was loaded up with goodies including a lobbied for provision reinstating financial practices causing the near apocalyptic financial collapse of 2008. The situation would be quite different if Directed eDemocracy were in place. **Directed eDemocracy changes the dynamics and**

culture of the legislative process. The Board would probably already have conducted advisory referendums substantiating the public's desire to move away from government by crisis, along with strategic views of taxation and entitlement reforms the public was open to. Faced with a public backlash against lawmakers not supporting Directed eDemocracy and responsiveness to voters, there would likely be nonpartisan progress on solving issues such as risky financial practices, and avoiding government by crisis leading to shut-down.

> In the US when pundits talk about "leadership" they usually do it in the context of a very limited number of great individual leaders such as Washington, Lincoln, or Roosevelt. "Leadership" is often associated with crisis, including war, along with manipulation of public opinion. In the context of Complex Adaptive Systems leadership is embedded in the system, where leadership is systematic adaptation to small crises without resorting to war and manipulation. **Directed eDemocracy is the basis for an adapting governmental system, which bolsters effective leadership and diminishes crisis and manipulation.**

In summation, we have problems that need solving, not the least of which is fixing a dysfunctional government that is unable to solve problems. In this Internet Age, we also have the opportunity of using new tools to create a Directed eDemocracy where citizens are not just consumers, but co-creators of government content. Our judicial system works well by putting courtroom trials to citizen juries. Should not our legislative system, driven mostly by partisan lawyers, not also be enabled to take legislative debates to citizen voters via referendum? Modern organizations run with an independent Board of Directors to represent stakeholders and attend to long term strategic matters. Should not our government also have an independent Board of Directors representing all citizens and attending to long term strategic matters? Directed eDemocracy offers all of the above, yet does it by starting in a low risk "advisory" manner responded to by an elected board of citizen problem solvers   limited to a single term of office.   Our representative democracy has continued to evolve for more than 200 years. Directed eDemocracy sets the direction for the next 200 years towards the ultimate hybrid "God" model capable of maximum cognition, foresight, and inviolate success in the global networked ecosystem of shared expectations.

To solve problems, compete, excel, and lead in this globalized internet age we want a government that is set up to provide the best cognition and adaptability possible for all stakeholders. Beyond that we do not want to let the personality of our government default to something we really don't want as a society. **In effect Directed eDemocracy changes the personality of our government.** We have "opened it up", and moved it out of the money'd special interest closed confines of Washington, and improved networked connections to all voters. We have thus made our government more "extroverted".   With direct connections to all voters, we have improved input and mitigated "blind spots".   We have thus made our government more "sensory". With an elected independent Board of Directors, we have added extra processing that can reconcile, and go beyond two opposing rigid "maps of the world". We have thus made our government more "thinking". By having a Board of Directors with voting privileges in the House and Senate we expand opportunities for effective action beyond partisan gridlock. We have thus made our government more "perceptive". **In Myers-Briggs personality parlance we have moved towards ESTP, which is "The Promoter".   According to Myers-Briggs, "Promoters" are good at making things happen, negotiating, trouble shooting, selling an idea or project, anticipating another's position, and conciliating. Sign me up – I want a government like that, and I hope after reading this book you do as well.**

SELECTED REFERENCES

Bartels, Larry M.: Unequal Democracy

Berggruen, Nicolas & Gardels, Nathan: Intelligent Governance for the 21st Century

Fossedal, Gregory: Direct Democracy in Switzerland

Friedman, Howard Steven: The Measure of a Nation

Garson, Barbara: Down the Up Escalator

Hirschhorn, Joel S.: Delusional Democracy

Johnson, Steven: Where Good Ideas Come From

kaufman, Stuart: At Home in the Universe

Leibovich, Mark: This Town

Liu, Eric & Hanauer, Nick: The Gardens of Democracy

McCullough, David: John Adams

Mitchell, Melanie: Complexity a Guided Tour

Paine, Thomas: Common Sense

Radigan, Dylan: Greedy Bastard$

Reich, Robert: Super Capitalism

Stockman, David : The Triumph of Politics

Surowiecki, James: The Wisdom of Crowds